Dramatic
and Symbolic Elements
in
Gregorian Chant

by Marie Pierik

DESCLEE COMPANY

NEW YORK — PARIS — TOURNAI — ROME — 1963

Library of Congress Catalog Card Number : 63-20670

Printed in Belgium

CONTENTS

ILLUSTRATIONS

5

640063

PREFACE

Many superlatives, both written and spoken, have been used in defining or describing the liturgical song called Gregorian Chant. An exhaustive amount of labor has been expended in the field of paleography in order to ferret out whatever existing amount of evidence may survive of this art of the Church in its original aspects. A tremendous amount of effort has also been put into melodic dissection of the chants, wherein comparative study has been made not only of different versions of the same melodies, but of various sections of the same as well. Many of these valuable works are highly illustrated with charts and diagrams, in which portrayals of the minutest details of the chant have been respected.

Certainly there is little to add to the learned achievements just described. However, there is one phase of the chant which I have long felt has not been developed to the extent that has been accomplished for other important features of it; that is, more intimate scrutiny of the composition and arrangement of the melodies in direct relation to the changing sentiment of the diverse texts with which they are allied. I do not mean to say that the average serious chant student does not dwell on the meaning of the texts being sung. Undoubtedly this requisite is clearly understood in general; but I doubt whether this aspect of the song is explored to the extent of adequate penetration into the song-writer's reason for using such-and-such a melodic line or note grouping, for selecting a particular style of chant, simple or florid, at given places, for choosing a certain tonality, etc., for *individual* expressive elements in the text.

In order to make my point clear I am going to picture the manner in which a serious student of classical secular music might go about analysis of, say, the first movement of a Beethoven Sonata or a Bach Fugue. First the student delves into the

7

ancestry of the piece through study of its preceding epochs of musical history, in order to determine to what extent the composition to be analyzed is a product of imitation of previous masters, or whether it is the genesis of a new and original manifestation of musical art. After this preliminary work comes analysis of the piece as a whole through dissection of its various parts, for realization of form and tonality, in following through the multiple tonal modulations and their logical reason for being.

The applied study just described brings the student to the threshold of the most important part of his search—the sentiment or mood which prompted the composer to choose a certain melodic line, be it one of height or depth, to determine the diverse length of phrases, and the transition from one tonality to another for the sake of appropriate "tonal color" at this or that place of his story in music. Added to this is the author's use of ornamental note inventions for particular expressive elements, and the thousand-and-one factors which enter into any work of art as a living expression of thought or sentiment. By this time the student has virtually memorized the composition, and nothing is left but that it become part of *his* being in execution.

Now let us return to the official music of the Church and compare the type of analytic work we chant students do in this sphere. I feel sure that we can all admit that a great deal of time and study is expended on Gregorian Chant with factors that are given undue consideration compared to that accorded other essentials which enter into the nature and being of the subject, and which fundamental elements are often less scrutinized than are only certain of its qualities.

One may object that an analytic approach to this art—and all that that implies—is "making the chant too difficult." Nevertheless, if a chant teacher neglected a serious academic approach to this subject, he would scarcely be qualified for imparting permanent knowledge of it to others. Here it might be added that acquired knowledge of this art coupled with bestowed light produces finished results in teaching in a period so brief, and even with the most unpretentious of students, as often to astonish the teacher himself. On the other hand, the " general aspect " approach more often produces the same quality of execution day after day, perhaps not bad, but certainly not finished unless it be for temporary spurts of improvement due to physical conditions or stimulating occasions.

There is another viewpoint to add to the foregoing : One may say, " It is all very well to dedicate even a lifetime of analytic work to the great music classics, for they contain an inexhaustible amount of matter that justifies this labor, whereas the chant pieces are but unpretentious melodies, simple for the most part, shorn of all the intricacies of composition that would justify an undue amount of applied study from the standpoint of musical composition alone. "

However, it is precisely the fact that these little works *are* unpretentious from the standpoint of involved workmanship that characterizes this product of a unique skill as the finest example of scientific and harmonious craftmanship that the world has ever produced in the marriage of word and melody, and at times within the span of from four to six diatonic notes. " That training is the most intricate that leads to the utter simplicity of a tune. " (Tagore) Close analysis of, and intimate association with these dramatic modulations more and more confirm in the mind their title to a durability that has not only lived centuries longer than any other form of music in Occidental history, but which has become ever more vital and revered in so doing.

A further point should also, I believe, be added to that which has already been said. Nowadays we hear critical evaluation of the traditional chants, brought out by musicologists in the liturgical field. These scholars are laying stress on the fact that in the Vatican 1907 edition of the Gradual, and perhaps other liturgical song books as well, the melodies are not always conserved in their entire integrity. In other words, there is a note here and there that should be changed, added or eliminated.

While conceding to the necessity of this scholarly research for the sake of arriving at a more perfect knowledge of this traditional art at its source, I wonder whether the average chant

9

student is not apt to be " thrown off the track " through these speculations if they become unduly preponderant in his eyes and lead him to the conclusion that it is not worth while for him to study the chant melodies too closely, because " they're all going to be changed anyway. "

Nothing could be more misleading than the impression just stated. Should it so occur that at some future time a revised Vatican edition of the chant melodies might appear, we can rest assured that the changes wrought in any such publications would be of minor significance compared to the wealth of art and science embodied in the Vatican Gregorian Chant editions as they now stand. If a student has arrived at a fundamental grasp of the latter, it will be a simple task later on to rectify accidental aspects in this regard. There is sufficient of beauty and truth in the melodies as they now are to fill a lifetime of fruitful study. So let us not be perturbed through groundless misgiving regarding the value of this sacred music in its present aspect.

Some of these songs originated in the time of Ambrose or during the epoch of the early Roman chant, with additions in a post-Gregorian period, a fact now granted by all scholars in the field of liturgical music. The final form of these plainchant melodies was very probably effected during the eight and ninth centuries through a fusion of Roman and Frankish elements, as a result of the Gallican elements which became infused into the Roman liturgy during the period of the Carolingian dynasty, which fusion remained in the liturgical books after their return to Rome.

But whenever or wherever this sacred song may have been produced, it is evident that it was effected by men whose awesome labor was void of worldly recognition during their mortal lives. Like the creations of their colleagues in other crafts, mosaic, sculpture and architecture, no names were signed to these masterpieces of early medieval art. Our chant authors filled the role of docile servants of God who acted as instruments under guidance of the Holy Spirit. And herein lies the intrinsic *nature* of these inspired modulations of prayer and drama, forerunners of celestial song.

M. P.

Since the reproduction of all the pieces analyzed in this study would entail a volume of considerable size and cost, for reference purpose the Solesmes-Desclée *Liber Usualis* (any recent edition) is employed as an edition commonly used by chant students. As each piece is announced, the text indicates the page where it is to be found.

INTRODUCTION

The Greek word for art *(technè)* signifies "means." There are two classes of art, the utilitarian arts, those which serve as means of sustenance for the body, and the liberal arts, those which serve as means of sustenance for the soul.

Music (Gr. *musikos*, belonging to the Muses) is a liberal art expressed in two manners, dramatic and symphonic. Dramatic music issued from the rhythm of the spoken and sung word, and terminated in the opera. Symphonic music issued from the rhythm of the bodily movements which accompanied primitive folk-song with instrumental accompaniment, and terminated in the developed expression of all instrumental music as we have it today.

Gregorian Chant, nucleus of Occidental song, is essentially a dramatic music. The origin of its melody is found in the *word*. Each simple and composite word has a distinct *rhythm*. In its smallest expression, word rhythm consists in the manner in which words and syllables are divided, and in its larger expression in the manner in which word combinations, or divisions, are proportioned, or comparatively related.

In reverting to the origin of simple words we discover that the element of rhythm embodied in their being resides in *variation in the quality of sound* among the various syllables of these words. There is one syllable in each word toward to and from which the remaining syllables tend in an effect of *crescendo* or *decrescendo*. This syllable is called the *tonic* (L. *tonus*, tone or sound) syllable of the word, as result of the musical tone accorded its accent (Gr. *pros*, to + *ode*, song; L. *ad*, to+*cano*, sing) by Greek and Latin orators of the classic age. In addition, the Greek words *arsis* (rise) and *thesis* (fall), applicable to bodily movements which accompanied lyric poetry in the ancient Greek play, were retained for the rise and fall of the

13

voice in oratorical discourse. Aristides Quintilianus, a musical theorist who lived before the middle of the third century, defines rhythm as " an ensemble of beats which follow one another according to a certain order. It is characterized by what is called *arsis* and *thesis*, noise and silence. " The word " silence " is used here only in a comparative sense : a soft *thesis* as compared with a vital *arsis*.

The Roman accent was vested with a certain *energy*, unknown to the Greeks, whose accent Cicero describes as " a less brilliant chant, a smothered tone. " Also, as Dom Joseph Pothier points out, the Latins " sang " less than the Greeks in discourse. With the Latins the *accentus* is the variety of *intensity* as much as, if not more than, the variety of pitch in the emission of verbal sound.

When the Latin language was established as a medium of Roman Catholic worship, not later than the fourth century, the phenomenon of tonal elevation on the accent became submitted uniquely to the empire of pitch, leaving the quality of intensity alone to act as generator of the rhythm of the word. Thus the term " tonic accent, " with no relation to pitch but rather to a dynamic element, will be used in this latter sense throughout this study. At the same time it is understood that the role of the tonic accent is to be considered in chant as one of *influence*—not of law. Our ancient composers were governed by the element of proportion, not rule.

We return then to the word as starting point for dramatic music : " Recitation is at the beginning and end of all genuine song, from the Psalms of the Hebrews to Gregorian Chant, and from the Greeks to Wagner " (Franz Boehme). Not only did the notes of syllabic chant (where one note or a simple neum accompanies each syllable) pattern their melodic line around the rhythm of the words, but the latter served as well for the rhythm of the neums, note groupings in melismatic, or florid, chant : " This chant, because of the close adaptation of the melody to the text, is not only most intimately conformed to the words, but also in a way interprets their force and efficacy

14

and brings delight to the minds of the hearers. "[1]

In study of origins in the realm of liturgical plainchant, one must continually revert to Greco-Roman sources. A history professor once commented that there is something implicit in the fact that God decreed the Incarnation of His Divine Son at the moment in history and at the place which put the whole of Greek and Roman culture at the disposition of the Christian tradition.

The short four and five note scales of ancient Greece are called tetrachords (Gr. *tettares*, four + *chorde*, string or chord) and pentachords (Gr. *penta*, five + *chorde*, string or chord). The conjunction of tetrachords and pentachords created a perfect unmodulating system of scales which passed through Greco-Roman music into the Middle Ages, when the ecclesiastical scales were established. The first evidence of the Church Modes is found in a collection of liturgical chants, either composed or compiled by St. John of Damascus (d.c. 770), which opus carries the title *Octoechos* (Eight Modes), and is modeled after the original work of Severus, Patriarch of Antioch (5th c.).

The Aeolian was the common scale of Greco-Roman music : *a*-A in descending order. The natural descent of the voice from a given pitch is a sequence of two single whole-steps followed by a half-step : 1-1-½. In taking as starting point the modern diapason, the first *a* above middle C, the tonic of the Aeolian Greek Mode, without pretending that it is necessarily the same pitch as our modern diapason, the sequence just described is obtained : *a*GlF½E, the tetrachord employed for the lower range of a number of early Church chants and recitatives. For the upper range of these melodies an analogous tetrachord closest to the model one evolves, but in ascending order : Gl*alb*½c. The conjunction of these tetrachords, both in ascending order, produces the following combination : E½FlGl*a*+Gl*alb*½c. Through elimination of the repeated notes the following hexachord (Gr. *hexa*, six + *chorde*, string or chord) is produced : E½FlGl*alb*½c. This is a varied interval setting from Guido's

[1] Pope Pius XII, *Musicae Sacrae Disciplina*, III.

later constructed hexachords, wherein but one half-step occurs, between the third and fourth notes. The hexachord described above actually comprises the first six notes of the Jewish scale for the chant of the Pentateuch, the Greek Dorian (in ascending order), and the established Church Phrygian scales. It is precisely this six-note scale, in whole or in part, that we observe in the melodic structure of the first altar and other liturgical chants: the *Páter nóster*, Preface, *Te Déum*, *Glória* of the Ambrosian Mass, etc.

PART ONE

EARLY ALTAR CHANTS AND TE DEUM

PREFACE FOR THE FEAST OF THE HOLY TRINITY AND SUNDAYS THROUGHOUT THE YEAR

The Preface is of very ancient order. In a certain sense it dates from before Christianity, since it was said by the Jews before the Paschal repast to thank God for His benefits to the Jewish people since the creation.

VERSES AND RESPONSES

Solemn Tone

Before going into analysis of chant pieces, it should be made clear that use of the modern musical terms " supertonic, mediant, subdominant, etc. " for modal scale pitches is merely a means of pointing out more conveniently the scale degrees of the latter, without meaning of identity, properly speaking.

In examining the alliance of the before-described hexachord with the words of the verses and responses which precede the Preface proper, it is seen that the initial note of the hexachord, E, works up in the nature of a Psalm Tone intonation, through G, modal mediant of E, where it accompanies the tonic accent of *ómnia*. The intonation then continues upward to *b*, original dominant of the E modal Church scale, where it supports the tonic accent of *saécula*, summit of the melodic arch. The tonic accent of *saeculórum* is strongly retained with the *clivis a*-G, *a* as note of unrest which resolves on the consonant note G. The latter is repeated for the tonic accent of *Amen* and the first

17

note of the *podatus* G-*a* on its atonic syllable. This suspensive cadence is an apt setting for this Latinized-Hebrew word, whose native accent is on the last syllable. Through absence of the note F the tritone F-*b* is avoided. The question of the tritone will be explained later.

The second verse and response use the modal G and *b* respectively for the two tonic accents. The final note of both the verse and response, *a*, is in each case a repetition of the second note of the preceding *clivis*, *b-a*. In the original E mode *a* demands resolution. It finds this for the verse on the first note of the following response, G. The response awaits its note of resolution until the final G of the following verse.

In the third verse the tonic accent of *Súrsum* soars up appropriately on a characteristic *quilisma*, *a-b-c*, to the highest note of the hexachord, lending beautiful variety to the modulation as well. The tonic and atonic accents of *chórda* undulate in contrary movement on the *podatus a-b* and the *clivis a-*G respectively. The response uses the same melodic setting as its verse, but in addition includes an appoggiatura (preceding ornamental note), *b*, and two notes of repetition for the three syllables in excess of its verse.

For the fourth and last verse the accompanying note of the first tonic accent, on *Grátias*, is varied through the use of *b*, followed by the ever artistic contrary movement of two neums, the *clivis a-*G and *podatus* G-*a*, one for the breve, the other for the atonic syllable. The characteristic *quilisima a-b-c* is accorded the tonic accent of *agámus*. The remainder of the verse repeats the first six notes of its own verse, with a repeated note for an extra syllable. The varied setting of the aforesaid *clivis* and *podatus* in their repetition is due to the variance between the two sets of verbal rhythms. The last word of the verse, *nóstro*, is rounded off with the *podatus a-b* on its tonic syllable, returning to *a* for its final syllable. The latter note resolves with the last note of the response, G. This response is a melodic repetition of the third one, with elimination of the appoggiatura of the latter, to correspond to one less syllable in the fourth response.

Both the Solemn and Simple Prefaces are composed within the G-*c* tetrachord described in the Introduction of this study. The number of periods, or full-stops, varies from two to five in both the Solemn and Simple Prefaces.

The lowest note of the tetrachord, G, is used only at the places of final cadence in both the Solemn and Simple Prefaces, and for the first note of the *podatus* on *ideo* in the Solemn Prefaces. The *clivis* a-G occurs either five or six syllables before the end of the period, depending on whether the final tonic accent is either two or three syllables before the close. The *podatus a-b* accompanies not only the final tonic accent before the full-stops, but the final tonic accent of all the phrases as well. The uniformity of these cadences reflects the majestic serenity of the text itself.

In the Simple Prefaces G as single note occurs on the fourth or fifth syllable before the full-stop, depending on whether the final tonic accent, which is always accompanied by *b*, is either two or three syllables before the close.

The characteristic quilisma *a-b-c* is present in all the Solemn Prefaces other than that of the Holy Trinity. Otherwise, this ornamental neum is used, but rarely, in the midst of the text, on the first tonic accent of a phrase, and is always found on the first accent (tonic for *súpplici*, rhythmic for *síne*) of the last phrase of the text.

Also wherever the word *Christum* preceded by *per* occurs the *quilisma* graces its tonic accent.

If the oft-quoted story that attributes to Mozart the confession that he would have exchanged all his compositions for the satisfaction of having composed the Roman Preface is but a pious legend, the fact still remains that this lyric praise of celestial glory, a melodic and textual flow of perfect symmetry—all expressed with but four diatonic notes—is a song of such elevating power, that no receptive participant of the Holy Sacrifice can listen to a well-delivered rendition of it without experiencing a quickening of spirit and an enlivenment of soul.

PRÆFATIO DE SANCTISSIMA TRINITATE

Per óm-ni - a sǽ-cu - la sæ-cu-ló - rum. ℞. A-men.

℣. Dó-mi-nus vo-bís-cum. ℞. Et cum spí - ri - tu tu - o.

℣. Sur-sum cor-da. ℞. Ha-bé-mus ad Dó-mi - num.

℣. Grá - ti - as a - gá-mus Dó-mi - no, De - o no-stro.

℞. Dig-num et ju-stum est. Ve-re dignum et ju-stum est,

æquum et sa-lu - tá - re, nos ti-bi semper et u-bí-que

grá-ti - as á-ge-re: Dó-mi-ne sancte, Pa-ter omní-po-tens,

æ-térne De-us: Qui cum u-ni-gé-ni-to Fí-li-o tu-o

et Spí-ri-tu Sancto unus es De-us, u-nus es Dómi-nus:

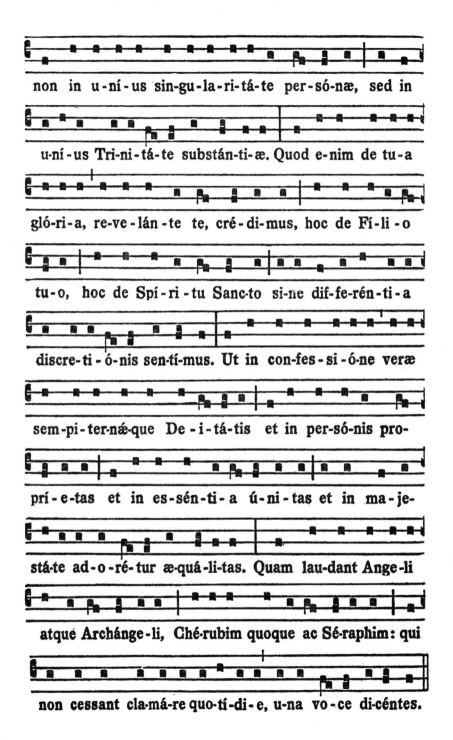

non in u-ní-us sin-gu-la-ri-tá-te per-só-næ, sed in

u-ní-us Tri-ni-tá-te substán-ti-æ. Quod e-nim de tu-a

gló-ri-a, re-ve-lán-te te, cré-di-mus, hoc de Fí-li-o

tu-o, hoc de Spí-ri-tu Sanc-to si-ne dif-fe-rén-ti-a

discre-ti-ó-nis sen-tí-mus. Ut in con-fes-si-ó-ne veræ

sem-pi-ter-næ-que De-i-tá-tis et in per-só-nis pro-

prí-e-tas et in es-sén-ti-a ú-ni-tas et in ma-je-

stá-te ad-o-ré-tur æ-quá-li-tas. Quam lau-dant Ange-li

atque Archánge-li, Ché-rubim quoque ac Sé-raphim: qui

non cessant cla-má-re quo-tí-di-e, u-na vo-ce di-céntes.

The foremost of the prayers of the Mass is the Lord's own, the *Páter nóster*. The Spanish Prudentius (Marcus Aurelius Clemens) of the fourth century, the oldest Church poet, says that the faithful said the *Páter noster* three times daily, providing this prayer as substitute for the three Jewish prayers of day and evening which implored the advent of the Messias, the Anointed.

In the early Church the *Pater* followed the Psalms and was really sung like them. St. Benedict prescribed it for the end of each Hour, and it is still solemnly sung by the Abbot or Prior, depending on the class of the feast, at Vespers and Lauds. It was in all the Mass liturgies, and a great number of the Fathers say it goes back to apostolic times. According to St. Jerome, it would have been Our Lord Himself who would have prescribed its use to the Apostles.

In the liturgies of the Orient and Paris (Gallican) the *Páter* was sung by the congregation. In the Mozarabic (Spanish) liturgy it was sung by the celebrant, but the congregation responded " Amen " after each phrase, with exception of the response " Quia Déus est " at one part. In Rome and Milan (through Roman influence) the *Páter* was sung by the celebrant, but the congregation responded with the " sed líbera nos a málo. "

The *Páter nóster* was placed between the Canon and *Fractio panis* by Gregory I, where it has retained its established position in the Roman rite. In the Mozarabic rite the *Páter nóster* is sung after the Communion, and the *Crédo* after the Consecration.

The first three petitions of the Lord's prayer have God Himself for object. The last four are devoted to man's spiritual and temporal needs in this life.

The melody of the *Páter nóster*, like that of the Preface proper, is comprised within the G-*c* tetrachord, with exception of the initial E of the last phrase sung by the celebrant. With inclusion of the response this song contains six periods, or full-stops, within ten phrases. The lowest note of the tetrachord, G, is used for the tonic accent of the opening word, *Páter*. This note then works up in psalmodic manner through its modal

First edition of the first printed Dominican Missal
(Venice : Octavianus Scotus, 1498).

mediant *b* on the tonic accent of *nóster*, to the tonally accented monosyllable *és* on *c*, highest note of the tetrachord, like a melodic aspiration to the Father who is in *heaven*. It then descends back in diatonic scale intervals to its starting point, G.

The reciting tone throughout the melody is the third tetrachord note *b*. The final accent of each of the phrases uses *a*, either singly or as first note of the *podatus a-b* on the tonic accent of *túum* and *térra*, or of the clivis *a-G* used before the two final full-stops. The last note of each of the ten phrases varies as follows : G-*a*-G-G-*a*-G-G-*a*-G-G.

Per ómni- a sǽ-cu- la sæ-cu-ló- rum. ℞. Amen. Jungit manus

O-rémus: Præ-céptis sa-lu-tá-ri-bus mó-ni- ti, et di-ví-na

insti-tu- ti- ó-ne formá- ti, audémus dí-ce-re : Extendit manus

Pa-ter noster, qui es in cæ-lis: sandi- fi-cé-tur nomen

tu-um: Advé-ni- at regnum tu-um: Fi-at vo-lúntas tu- a,

sic-ut in cæ-lo, et in terra. Pa-nem nostrum quo-ti-di- ánum

da no-bis hó-di- e: Et di-mít-te no-bis dé-bi-ta nostra,

sic-ut et nos dimít-timus de-bi-tó-ri-bus nostris. Et ne nos

indú-cas in tenta- ti- ó- nem. ℞. Sed lí-be-ra nos a ma- lo.

Sacerdos secrete dicit : Amen.

23

The ensemble of the melody is a veritable musical poem made up of three strophes, one of three verses and two of two verses, interspersed with one single verse and followed by two single ones.

The notes which accompany the tonic, secondary and rhythmic accents, together with the final notes of each phrase, are portrayed in the following diagram :

1. G-*b*-*c*-*a*-G *(mora vocis)*
2. *a*-*b*-G-*a*-*a* (pause)
3. *c*-*a*-*a*-G *(m. v.)*
4. *b*-*a*-*a*-G *(m. v.)*
5. *a*-*b*-G-*a*-*a* (pause)

6. G-*b*-*a*-*c*-*a*-*a*-G (pause)
7. *a*-*a*-*c*-*b*-*a*-G *(m. v.)*
8. *a*-*b*-*b*-G-*b*-*a*-*a* (pause)
9. E-*a*-*b*-*a*-*a*-G-*a*-G *(rallentando and pause)*

10. *a*-*a*-*a*-G *(rallentando)*

In solfaing these notes of accentuation, while at the same time observing the rhythmic punctuations parenthetically indicated, one better appreciates the skill with which this verbal accentuation is melodically varied within the confines of but a simple diatonic tetrachord.

Lastly, in singing the entire melody with its notes of passage, preparation, resolution, etc., at the same time conserving the rhythmic punctuation of the cadences, one perceives the beautiful effect produced through the varied accentual setting of but four diatonic notes, whose summit *c* appears at proportional intervals like an intermittent ray of light on the cross at the apex of a cathedral spire.

What maker of tunes could compare with the rare combination of vigor and serenity that permeates this marriage of word and melody through the ingenious operation of four simple notes!

Compare the manner in which the pentachord E-*b* is used

Mozarabic *Páter Nóster*

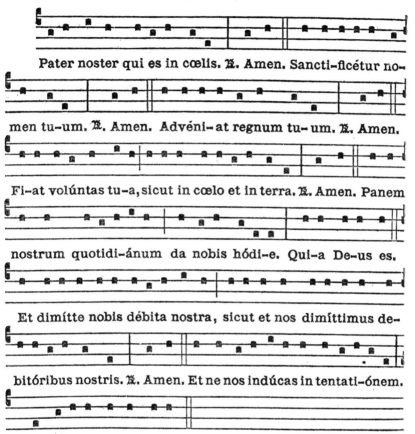

Pater noster qui es in cœlis. ℞. Amen. Sancti-ficétur no-

men tu-um. ℞. Amen. Advéni-at regnum tu-um. ℞. Amen.

Fi-at volúntas tu-a, sicut in cœlo et in terra. ℞. Amen. Panem

nostrum quotidi-ánum da nobis hódi-e. Qui-a De-us es.

Et dimítte nobis débita nostra, sicut et nos dimíttimus de-

bitóribus nostris. ℞. Amen. Et ne nos indúcas in tentati-ónem.

℞. Sed líbera nos a malo.

in the above illustration with its application to the *Glória* of
Roman Mass XV.

Eric Werner shows with demonstration that the melodic
formula of the latter chant, together with that of the *Te Déum*,
recurs almost literally in a Yemenite *Sh'ma* (the oldest chant
of Hebrew liturgy) and in a Yemenite cantillation of the Thora. [1]

[1] E. WERNER, " The Common Ground, " *Atti del Congressio Internationale
di Musica Sacra* (Rome, 1951), 10.

The *Te Déum*, one of the earliest of Christian songs, was composed by Nicetus, Bishop of the province of Dacia, around 400 A.D. There is no existing proof that the melody as we now have it is the original one, but at any rate it is a very old one, a flowering of the most ancient recitatives. The similarity of an old Hebrew chant to the *Te Déum* melody has just been pointed out. In the early Church the *Te Déum* was interchangeable with the *Glória* after Matins, both being hymns of praise to the Holy Trinity.

In its first stage the *Te Déum* probably ended after the word *numerári*. This verse is in the nature of an Antiphon, as in psalmody. The subsequent verses were added at later dates, in two different stages. For the purpose of our study we will use only the original section (1832).

The melody of the *Te Déum* is contained within the same hexachord as that of the verses and responses of the Preface : E-*c*, in avoiding F for the reason already pointed out in the Preface verses. All six of these notes appear in the opening theme, the first four notes of which are likewise those of the first four notes of the first Preface verse. The characteristic *quilisma a-b-c* of the same verses and responses occurs also in the *Te Déum*, designed as well for appropriate expression of the sentiment of the text. It is used first for the tonic accent of *laudámus* in the opening phrase; next as virile support for the tonic accents of the triple majestic *Sánctus*, the third one with inclusion of all the notes of the hexachord other than F. The *quilisma* is also employed for the tonic accents of the words *Pátrum* and *Sánctum*, as well as in four additional settings of the first theme.

The *Te Déum* comprises four themes : 1) *Te Déum laudámus ;* 2) *Te Déum confitémur ;* 3) *Te aetérnum Pátrum ;* 4) *Tu Rex glóriae*. With exception of the initial theme and the *quilisma* settings of the triple *Sánctus*, as also of the tonic accents of *Pátrum* and *Sánctum*, themes 2 and 3 are used consecutively for the two-part melodic sections until the appearance of theme 4.

At *Tu Rex glóriae* the Son is accorded a new theme, 4, used for the entire verse. The *Te Déum* motif is repeated for *Tu Pátris*, in conformity with the identity of the Person addressed. The *Tu Pátris* verse then continues with theme 4, interspersed with theme 1, which, from here on serves to proclaim the Divine Filiation, Incarnation, Redemption, Resurrection and Judgment of the Redeemer, a tremendous dramatic sequence expressed in a minimum of words for a maximum of power. The *Aetérna fac* portion with its new melody was probably used as an Antiphon as in psalmody.

The theme of the Son is appropriately applied for the *Júdex créderis* verse, awesome words of the coming of Christ as Judge. This is followed by the touching appeal of the *Te ergo* verse, contained in theme 1 for its first part. For its second part theme 4 is reserved, for here the Savior is reminded of the price He has paid for man's redemption—the shedding of His Precious Blood.

In this hymn of praise we find the unusual achievement of a hymn of twenty verses composed with four main melodic themes not in consecutive order as in established hymnody form, but in diverse settings with particular application of each theme for various verse texts. In addition we discover other interesting particularities. For example, the characteristic *quilisma* accords an initial element of uplift to the final tonic syllable of theme 1 in its first appearance, and is also reserved for dramatic settings where they are called for; skillful manipulations are managed for use of the same theme for diverse texts, as in places where a *podatus* and its following *punctum* used for a verse of greater length become a *torculus* for a shorter verse, while a repeated note in the former is eliminated in the later. (See *Pléni sunt caéli et térra* and *Te gloriósus*.) Again, a shorter text may do without the intonation of a longer one and start right in on the reciting note. (See *Apostolórum chórus* and *majestátis glóriae.*)

27

When we consider that the amount of melodic matter at the disposition of a composer or adapter, as the case may be, is nothing beyond a six-note diatonic scale for providing a musical consort worthy of the exalted magnitude of a *Te Déum* text and admit that this claim has been fulfilled to the point of perfect satisfaction, we are at liberty to state that this magnificent laudation of song carries with it the stamp of highest integrity and musicianship for its epoch.

PART TWO

OFFICE ANTIPHONS

THE ANTIPHON

History

For origin of the word " antiphon " we return again to Greece : *antiphonos, anti* (against) + *phone* (sound). In ancient Greece every sung piece was preceded by an instrumental prelude, whose object it was to impress upon the mind of the auditor, and executant himself, the Tone or Mode of the vocal melody. The Greek term *endosium* (L. *exordium*, beginning) is often used by Aristotle, always with the meaning of a beginning, an entrance into matter. When the Church adopted collective psalmody, a musical formula of the same kind became indispensible for indicating to the chorus of faithful the air and diapason of the Psalm to be sung. Instruments not having access to the sanctuary, their role passed to the precentor, and the prelude transformed itself into the Antiphon. The latter served also as terminating formula. The repetition of the Antiphon after the doxology dates from the primitive epoch of the Church.

The most ancient account in which the Antiphon and Psalms are separately enumerated is found in the story of a certain Egeria, possibly a nun of Gaul, author of *Peregrinatio ad loca sancta* (c. 385-388), who heard the Psalms sung by two alternate choirs at Jerusalem. This mode of singing was inherited from the Synagogue, where men's voices alternated an octave apart with a chorus of women's and children's voices. From the Eastern Church it was introduced into the Latin Church at Milan the latter part of the fourth century, when St. Ambrose taught his congregation the rendition of psalmody and hymnody.

The Antiphons possess a freedom of style all their own. The Antiphon grew out of the *melody* rather than out of the *recitative*, the latter as origin of responsorial chant.

The responsorial, antiphonal and tract songs of Gregorian Chant comprise three processes of composition : 1) Original melodies; 2) Melodies of adaptation; 3) Melodies of centonization.

The number of Antiphons in the liturgy far exceed any other type of chant. The original melodies of the Roman Antiphonary are contained in the *Tonarius* of Regino, Abbot of Prüm (d. 951), an Antiphon collection anterior to certain modal alterations. It comprises the earliest collection for exploration for the some thirteen hundred Antiphons sung in the daily Office. Included in process 1 in this vast collection there are forty-seven themes, each of which includes a varying number of Antiphons. However, there are but thirty-four themes and four variants which Auguste Gevaert considers as primitive, and therefor *original*, and which he attributes to Greco-Roman origin. In his important work *La Mélopée Antique dans le Chant de l'Église Latine*, [1] Gevaert concentrates particularly on study of the Office Antiphons.

In process 2 of composition, adaptation, this procedure is always executed with a like type of piece : Antiphon to Antiphon, Introit to Introit, Communion to Communion, etc. However, the same text can be adapted to two different types of pieces, as we shall later observe.

When in adaptation the original melody is modified, this is done in order to conserve the sentiment and length of the new text, and also to respect variance from the original in the adapted verbal accentuation : " If one examines attentively the appropriation of a unique melody, or *timbre*, to different words, it is proved that this has not been done by chance—far from it! The music of the *timbre* is, for the most part, subject not only to the meaning of the text, but to the accents of the words as well, so is consequently modified. There is change of music when there is change of sentiment or of accentuation. All the

[1] (Ghent : Ad. Hoste, 1895).

30

dramatic principles are there. Besides, use of the *timbre* is most often limited to texts which, although different, refer to a general identical sentiment " (Vincent d'Indy).

Process 3 of composition, centonization, is a procedure used for compositions constructed of passages of chant chosen from one or more existing pieces, and put together in a manner that distinguishes them from the original compositions. This process occurs most frequently in the Graduals, the Tracts and the Responsories of Matins. In addition, centonization is used to a degree in the Office Antiphons. In his *Estetica Gregoriana* Dom Ferretti gives a table of seventeen formulae for Antiphons of the first Mode and a list of thirty-two melodies composed from these formulae. This estimate is, however, modified by Willi Apel, who points out that Ferretti's material is not taken from a special " theme group " but is selected from all the Antiphons of the first Mode, more than 330 in number, of which Ferretti's list represents less than one-tenth. At the same time, several of the melodies are examples not of centonization, but of complete adaptation. Apel substantiates this statement with a list of Antiphons with their adaptations, such as, *Súbiit ergo* (564), *Mulíeres sedéntes* (738), *Omnes qui habébant* (1091), *Qui non cólligit* (556) and others. However, there still remain a number of Antiphons showing true centonization, various combinations of fixed phrases, among which the *Liber Usualis* contains the following : *Qui vérbum Déi* (504), *Córpora sanctórum* (1153), *Quaérite prímum* (1040), *Visiónem* (550), *Qui me mísit* (1085) and four additional Antiphons in the Antiphonary. [1]

Gevaert considers that the origin of the text is in general a criterion for determining the time of adoption of any certain Antiphon into the Office. He places the Office Antiphons in the three following categories :

I. a) Antiphons vocalized on the word *Allelúia*. (See Sunday Little Hours, Paschal Time 229 ff.) b) Psalmodic Antiphons, comprising all the melodies of the Antiphonary in

---

[1] *Gregorian Chant* (University of Indiana Press, 1958), pp. 402-403.

which the words are taken from the Psalm or Canticle to which
it is joined. (See Vespers for Sundays and Ferial Days, 250 ff.)
The Antiphons of this category remount to the first organization
of the Hours and are the kind that were used at the time when
St. Benedict redacted his Rule (toward 530).

II. In this category are Antiphons taken from biblical
writings other than the Psalms : Books of the Prophets, Wisdom,
historical texts, and, by exception, texts borrowed from ancient
Christian literature. This group of Antiphons replaced the
primitive type. They fill more than three-fourths of the daily
office, and came into full development from 540-600, when
the last of pagan institutions had disappeared in the Occident.
These chants developed in the shadow of the Church of Rome,
which at that time already possessed a poetry and music adapted
to its cult—an *original* art, with inherited characteristics but
new in form and tendencies, which sprang from the heart of
Christian society. Gevaert calls the Antiphons of this period
the " veritable jewels of the Antiphonary. " (See Vespers
for the first Sunday of Advent, 323 ff.)

III. In the last category are texts borrowed from *Gesta
Martyrum* of *Passiones* (Acts of the Martyrs), or from the lives
of saints already honored at Rome by a particular cult : St. Agnes,
St. Agatha, St. Cecilia, St. Andrew, St. Martin of Tours, etc.
(See Vespers of SS. Lucy, Agnes, Agatha, 1324, 1340, 1370).
Because of their extraction these texts could not have been
introduced into the Roman cursus before the seventh century,
since pontifical decrees of the preceding century prohibited
usage of this sort of writing in the Divine Office. A Roman
document contemporary with *Liber Pontificalis* (toward 520)
declares that the reading of *Gesta Martyrum* was prohibited
in Rome in reunions of the cult. Besides, a letter of St. Gregory,
redacted in 598, states that he himself completely ignored this
branch of Christian literature.

Among the Antiphons of the third category are included
those of the four Feasts of the B.V.M., which were established
in Rome in the seventh century. There are no Antiphons

in this category whose basic themes have not been derived from the two preceding ones.

Gevaert bases the above division of texts upon the premise of the melodic material. He points out that thirty-four out of his forty-seven themes occur with texts from each of the three categories, and that the Antiphons with psalmodic texts are of a more simple and concise character. He at the same time asks whether it can be said that we possess the Antiphons from the middle of the fourth to the end of the seventh century. He then answers his own query : " If we compare the ninth and tenth century Antiphons with those of today, we discover that the great majority of Antiphons are sung to the same suave melodies as around nine hundred, except for slight deformations like those seen today from one collection to another. Very rarely has the text received a different modulation or has the chant been disfigured in a manner to become unrecognizable.

" All in keeping their pattern, a certain number of melodies have modified their harmonic structure or changed their Modes.... Most of the altered melodies belong to the same modal forms and to the same nomic themes. Besides, in analyzing them with care we soon recognize that these alterations are not, for example, the result of fault of memory of the singers or of accidents impossible to verify, but are due to musical causes very comprehensible to us : the tendency to avoid awkward intonations of the voice; confusion between similar themes. Ultimately we see changes produced with striking uniformity.

" On the other hand, intense examination of the most recent documents shows that already at the time of their redaction perturbing causes had agitated for quite a long time and had determined certain modal alterations identical to those that are attributed to more recent epochs.... This permits us to recognize the changes which happened at some certain epoch, but which did not touch the sources. Furthermore, it permits us to discern with surety the melodies which have remained pure of all alterations since their birth. " [1]

[1] GEVAERT, *op. cit.*, pp. 161 ff.

33

In broad lines two types of form obtain in the melodies of liturgical plainchant : 1) Those constructed under the form of simple psalmody, the pieces of the Proper of the Mass; 2) Those constructed under the style of freedom of form, the Antiphons and Responsories of the Office.

In the first category the psalmodic form of intonation, tenor, or reciting tone, temporary cadence or cadences, and final cadence, are distinguishing features. In the second category these features are still present, but not necessarily so clearly defined as in the pieces constructed on the formula of simple psalmody. A relatively greater variety of intervals, and at the same time expressive elements with shorter motives, occur in pieces of the second category than in those of pure psalmodic form. We shall observe these characteristics in analysis of the Antiphons themselves.

One of the features of a number of early Church Antiphons is the symmetry of their melodic construction, a characteristic of the symmetrical form of ancient Greek poetry : a strophe of four verses in which the members are almost equal, with a voice suspension after each member. As regards the Antiphon melodies themselves, however, an authority on Greek music stresses that it is less than probable that the Christians used the Greek nomes (*timbres*, fixed melodies). For those who knew their minds, it is apparent that it would be impossible for them to use foreign melodic forms, but they could imitate them and they did (Amédée Gastouée).

A classic example of the symmetry just described is found in the Antiphon *Ecce sacérdos mágnus* (1176), which includes number 23 of Gevaert's 47 themes. Some thirty Antiphons employ this same theme. *Ecce sacérdos mágnus* consists of four phrases, or members, three of which comprise seven syllables. One phrase, the second, has but five syllables. Each syllable of the seven-syllable phrases is accompanied by but one note (syllabic chant). The five-syllable phrase follows the same procedure except for two of its syllables, each one of which has two notes, that which completes its seven-note setting and results in the same number of notes for each of the four phrases of the piece. Here the periodicity of the reposes, approximate to the diverse length of the melodies, is the same as in the Greek hymn. See also Antiphon *Véni spónsa* (1214).

(In subsequent use of the word "modulation" this is, of course, completely foreign to the meaning of harmonic modulation as employed in modern music. In the following modal melodies the term is used to signify the termination of melodic divisions on particular degrees of the modal scale.)

The melodic form of the Antiphons consists of four types :
1) A nomic form without note modulation. (See *Laetátus sum*, 282.)
2) The binary type : two phrases separated by one note modulation. For example, the little Antiphon *Sit nómen Dómini benedíctum* (254) consists of two melodic members with one intervening note modulation, to *c*, subdominant of G, tonic of mode 7. The first phrase is Gevaert's number 23 of his 47 themes.
3) The ternary type consists of three phrases separated by two note modulations. In the Antiphon *Phillipe qui vídet me* (1451) the first short member modulates to *d*, dominant of G, tonic of Mode 7; the second phrase modulates to *c*, subdominant of the same Mode. The ternary form is the modern Lied type, brought to established development in the Beethoven Andante movement.
4) The quatenary type is comparatively rare among the Antiphons : four phrases with three intervening note modulations. If in a four-phrase song one of the melodic members is reapeated, this is actually a ternary type. The Antiphon *Némo te condemnávit* (558) is a quatenary type. The first note modulation is to G, modal mediant of E, tonic of Mode 3; the second is to *b*, original dominant of the same Mode; the third is to *c*, submediant and later established dominant of Mode 3. We shall refer again to the tonality of this piece.

The *incipit* (beginning) and cadence (close) of the Antiphons

35

are very important factors in its melodic construction.   As
originally used the *incipit* had been all important for establishing
the tonality of the piece.   But when in the tenth and eleventh
centuries the custom came about of repeating only the last part
of the Antiphon text intercalated between the Psalm verses,
the *vox finalis* (end) of the Antiphon became the determinate
factor for indicating the Mode, or tonality, of the piece.

The transition from the final of the Psalm Tone into the
intonation of the Antiphon, and vice versa, produces an artistic
union of the Antiphon with the dominant of the Psalm Tone.
When a Psalm is sung with an Antiphon, the final of each is
adapted to the intonation of the other.   That is the reason for
the various Psalm endings (indicated by the vowels EOUAE
found in the last words of the doxology), chosen to lead smoothly
into the Antiphon which follows.   In general the number of
terminations provided for a given Tone agree with the number
of incipits found among Antiphons of the same Mode.

The initial interval of an intonation can never be more than
a fifth, and this interval can be used only from the tonic of the
Mode.   It is therefore not for all Modes.   A very important
incipit of this kind is that of Mode 1 : D-*a*-b♭-*a*, frequently
employed in chant pieces of this modality.   It is customary for
this interval used as an intonation to be preceded by an ornamental
preparatory note or notes. (See Antiphons *Erunt práva*, *Técum
princípium*, *Collígite prímum*, *Ave María*, etc., 357, 412, 494, 1416.)
There are, however, exceptions to this procedure, as, for example,
in the Antiphon *Símile est* (495).   Dom Morin states that b♮,
not b♭, belongs to the tonality when this intonation is used in
Mode 4.   It is so conserved in the Hebrew Pentateuch Mode.
This change would effect chant pieces such as *Quid fáciem* (1016)
and the Introit *Sálus pópuli* (1059).

The b♭ was introduced into this motif in order to avoid
a covered tritone : F-G-*a*-*b*, three consecutive whole-tones,
called by medieval musicologists the " diabolus in musica. "
Nevertheless, the covered tritone existed as late as the ninth
century.   According to Gevaert there are twenty instances
of it in the Regino Antiphonary.   (See the last four syllables

of the intonation *Ecce Dóminus véniet,* 324.) The Greeks used the tritone, but it became rarer with the approach of modern times. Gevaert considers its traditional mutation in liturgical plainchant as a veritable dissolution of the ancient melodies. The Benedictines have largely reinstated the *b♮* in their editions.

The *b♮* or *b♭* are used also in cases of transposition. If a chant melody is raised a fourth, as the tonic E of Modes 3 and 4 to *a*, or the tonic of Mode 8, G, to *c*, a *b♮* in the transposed version indicates an F♯ in the original melody. If a melody is raised a fifth, as the tonic of Modes 1 and 2, D, to *a*, or the tonic of Mode 4, E, to *b*, or the tonic of Mode 6, F, to *c*, this indicates in the transposed version a b♭ in the original melody.

Chromatics, such as E♭ and F♯, probably used in the original tonal system, were never used by medieval theorists. In fact the ancient neum manuscripts in open space did not even use the b flat.

The *incipit* described above, D-*a*-*b♭*-*a*, was later employed in original or transposed form by composers of the polyphonic, classical and modern epochs. Vittoria uses it in his Motet *O vos omnes;* it is the subject theme in the Bach E♭ minor Clavicord Fugue (Book I); Gabriel Fauré employs it in the vocal quartet " Madrigal, " and it is found in a theme of Meyerbeer's *Les Hugenots,* to mention only particular cases (d'Indy).

In some cases the Antiphon *incipit* of a direct fifth in the first Mode is followed by a minor third, as in *Vádo ad éum* (825), *Fóntes et ómnia* (884), *Vos amíci* (1111), etc. For Mode 7 see the same combination in the Antiphon *Urbs fortitúdinis* (332). The *incipit* of a major fifth and a minor third is frequently interspersed with intermediary notes, as in the Antiphon *Dóminus véniet* (357).

It is very fine art to arrive at the end of a chant melody in gradual and sequent manner. This is portrayed throughout Gregorian Chant in general. A beautiful example of this voice leading occurs in the Antiphon *In velaménto clamábant* (1120), where the three final " allelúias " course down from *a*, dominant of Mode 1 (Authentic Mode of 2), to the final tonic D. Consummate artistry is revealed in the melodic variety of this

thrice-uttered acclamation of joy. The first " allelúia " is adorned
with two neums, one in descending, the other in ascending
contrary movement; the second " allelúia " progresses downward
through a two-fold *clivis*, while the third rises a minor third
from the modal tonic and then descends in scale intervals back
to the tonic. Herein is found the most skillful variety possible
of three melodic settings of the same word, effected within the
span of a minor seventh. The notes which accompany the tonic
accents of the three-fold " allelúia, " G-F-D, become even more
effective through this *decrescendo* in the melody.

Leading tone cadences, possible only on F, are most unusual
in Gregorian Chant. Apel gives the only example in the *Liber
usualis* for the Antiphons, *Virgo pótens* (1679), and in the Roman
Antiphonary the Antiphon *O quam gloriósum.* [1]

The Antiphons make very restricted usage of ornamental
style. Even the vocalizations at either the end of the song or
at the conclusion of the phrases, as well as the melismatic passages
at the interior of the piece, are the result of the brevity of the
text. Their purpose is to establish a certain equilibrium between
the diverse parts of the melodic whole. Some Antiphons
composed in ornate style from one end to the other are found
in the long Antiphons of the Gospel Canticles, *Magníficat* and
Benedictus. (See *O Crux splendídior,* 1453.) However, these
songs do not incorporate the very developed vocalizations nor the
technical refinement of the Antiphons of the Mass.

Tonality

The Antiphons of the Roman Office comprise all the Eight
Church Modes, with the largest number in Modes 1 and 8.
Gevaert states that in the Tonarius of Regino, the Greek Aeolian
(tonic *a*) and Ionian (tonic G) Modes are used " in overwhelmingly
larger number than are the Greek Dorian (tonic E) and
Hypolydian (tonic F) Modes. " [2] The same authority asserts
that these four Greek Modes became the Authentic Ecclesiastical
Modes, whose tonics are D-E-F-G, respectively. In accordance

[1] W. APEL, *op. cit.*, p. 265.
[2] *Op. cit.*, p. 98.

with the same doctrine, the tonic D came about through transposition of the Aeolian Mode, thought upwards, four degrees higher, through which process the interval steps of the Aeolian Mode and its transposed version with ♭ flat are identical, both considered in ascending order. The remaining Greek Modes retained their original setting (but in ascending order), and became Church Modes 3, 5, 7. Although this theory is not accepted by all present day musicologists, it is a logical formula. Gevaert is also of the opinion that all the Church melodies could have been written in the Greek Aeolian and Ionian Modes, Ecclesiastical Modes 1 and 7, with their Plagals.

In this respect it is interesting to observe that the two basic tetrachords described in the introduction of this study : a-E in descending order and G-c in ascending order, are precisely those of the first transposed (from Aeolian) descending tetrachord of Church Mode 1 with b♭ : dlclb♭½a, and the first ascending tetrachord of Church Mode 7, Glalb½c. These two tetrachords are identical to the first Greek Aeolian tetrachord in descending order and the first Greek Ionian tetrachord in ascending order, the two Modes which Gevaert believes would have supplied the modal requirements of all liturgical chant.

The Peregrinus (strange) Tone, with its two dominants, a and G, is probably a heritage of the pre-Christian era. Eric Werner maintains that the *Tonus Peregrinus* of the *Antiphonale Sarisburiense* is identical tone for tone and note for note with the Hallel Tone of the Yemenite Jews—the same text with the same melody. [1]

The Peregrinus Tone is used for certain Antiphons, such as *Mártyres Dómini* (1154), *Angeli Dómini* (1660), *Laudáte púeri* (not contained in the *L.U.*), all with the same melody, which Antiphons have had their special psalmody for over eight hundred years. A noteworthy characteristic of this Tone is also the manner in which its intonation and termination formulae harmonize with the melody of the Antiphon itself. An example

[1] E. WERNER, *op. cit.*, p. 8.

39

of this is found in the fifth Psalm of Sunday Vespers, *In éxitu* (254), which uses the Peregrinus Tone.

The problem of modal assignment to any certain chant piece is one which apparently puzzled even the earliest musicologists, nor are they always in agreement concerning the designation of a particular Mode to one and the same piece. This uncertainty prevails to a degree throughout Gregorian Chant in the Mass Propers, but it is probably more pronounced in the Office chants. For example, in redaction of a melody there is sometimes change of Mode from the original designation, as in the Antiphon *Adhaésit ánima méa* (418), which was formerly considered as belonging to Mode 3, but which is now attributed to Mode 8. Both Modes have the same dominant, *c* (originally *b* in Mode 3). There is also similarity in the themes of the two Modes. In the Antiphon *Némo te condemnávit* (558), which we examined in the section on form, with its ever recurring G and *c*, tonic and dominant of Mode 8, the tonality of that Mode is also stressed during the course of the melody in addition to the cadence notes of Mode 3.

Adaptation

Before going into the subject of adaptation of melodies to new texts, it is well to preface this with the statement that in general the adaptations of the later so-called " Silver Age " are not considered as perfect from an analytic point of view as are the original chants of the so-called " Golden Age. " On the other hand, it is but just to concede that this later product, imperfect as it may appear in some particulars, carries with it no stamp of mediocrity. On the contrary, it is evident that the adapters of liturgical plainchant sought scrupulously throughout the texts and melodies of the already existing repertory before putting their finger on just the right melody for adaptation to a new text. Add to this that it is not entirely satisfying to judge these traditional chant adaptations on the basis of present-day developed theoretical standards, any more than it would be to judge the composition of the Bible by the standards of current knowledge of literature. In both cases it is necessary to see through the eyes of the past.

As Gevaert says in speaking of the Office Antiphons, the process of adaptation of the same melody to various texts is not the result of poverty of invention. For daily worship, and particularly for congregational song, repetition is valuable. The original composition and the adaptation may be considered as distinct, sometimes centuries apart.

Among the most widely used Antiphon melodies for adaptation are those of *Ecce véniet Prophéta mágnus* (324), which incorporates Gevaert's theme 29, and *Si vere frátres* (509), which includes Gevaert's theme 23, which melody we already know in the Antiphon *Ecce sacérdos mágnus* (1176). The first of these melodies appears about eighty times in the Antiphonary for Vespers and Lauds alone, and is frequently used at other times as well, and, as already stated, some thirty Antiphons employ theme 23. *Ecce véniet Prophéta*, with the last word substituted for *dominátor*, is the only Antiphon mentioned before the sixth century.

As preface to the matter of adaptation of the *Ecce véniet Prophéta* theme, something should be said about its tonality, which stands apart from the system of the Church Modes. Wagner considers that it is of non-liturgical origin. In the present Vatican Edition it is attributed to Mode 4. Were E to be retained as tonic without transposition an F$\sharp$ would be necessary on the first syllable of the word *renovábit*. The Antiphonary of Blessed Hartker (codices 390-391) of St. Gall ascribes it to Mode 4, as does the Montpellier *Tonale* of the eleventh century. Gevaert places it in Mode 7. The Cistercians use this latter Mode. This is a fair example of the diversity which may exist in modal assignment, although this is a particular case. In analysis we will consider the *Ecce véniet Prophéta* Antiphon as in Mode 4, in conformity with the Vatican Edition.

In comparison of 1) Antiphon *Ecce véniet Prophéta* with 2) Antiphon *Satiávit Dóminus* (563) in adaptation, it is seen that both pieces comprise four melodic phrases, or members.

However, within these phrases the number of syllables differs as follows : 1) 5, 5, 7, 8 versus 2) 7, 8, 6, 7.

In the first phrase of each piece the initial note G accompanies a verbal accent, tonic in 1, secondary in 2. Both intonations work up through *a* to *c*, the latter used as support for the final tonic accent in each intonation. The two extra syllables in 2 are provided for with two extra *c*s as single notes. Had the *podatus c-d* on the breve syllable of *véniet* in 1 been employed for the breve syllable of *Dóminus* in 2, the note *c* would have occurred here four consecutive times. This melodic monotony is skillfully avoided through substitution of the *podatus d-e* for the latter syllable. At the same time this melodic modification lends an added smoothness to the word *Dóminus* as well.

The number of syllables in the second phrase of each piece is : 1) 5 versus 2) 8. Each phrase has the same notes, but in view of the three extra syllables in 2, the two-note neums in 1 are used singly in 2, with an added *d*, dominant of the transposed Mode, at the final of its second phrase. The note *e*, summit of the transposed Mode, supports the tonic accent of the climatic word in each phrase, *Prophéta* in 1, *míllia* in 2.

In the third phrase the number of syllables in each piece is 1) 7 versus 2) 6. The opening single notes of 1, *a* and *d*, preceded by an *anacrusis* (" up-beat " note), are used as *podatus* in 2, while the *clivis a*-G of 1 is set as single notes in 2 on the first two syllables of *pánibus*. The last two verbal accents of each phrase, secondary in 1, tonic in 2, are accompanied by *b* and *a* respectively, the latter functioning strongly as tonic accent in the transposed Mode. The final note of 1, *a*, glides down to G on a *clivis* in 2, in order that the latter note may lead smoothly into F, initial note of the following phrase.

In the fourth and final phrase the number of syllables in each piece is 1) 8 versus 2) 7. The note F, dominant of transposed Mode 3 (Authentic of 4), accompanies the first verbal accent of each phrase, tonic in 1, rhythmic in 2. The preceding appoggiatura note in 1, G, lends particular emphasis to the F. The melody in 1 then moves up in scale intervals to *c* on the secondary accent of the word *allelúia*. Its corresponding piece does the same, except to substitute the single note on *a* on the tonic accent of *duóbus* for the *podatus a-b♭* on the atonic syllable of the word *Jerúsalem* in 1. Had the tonic accent of *duóbus* in 2 used the latter *podatus* at this place, it would have been unduly retarded in relation to the remaining chant setting. As it is, the transposed modal tonic *a* at this place acts as anticipation for its last and strongest appearance at the final of the cadence.

In neither of the above analyzed pieces is the number of syllables in both of the Antiphons the same. Nevertheless, not only has the same melody been used for each text, but in adaptation the same notes have been retained for verbal accentuation, despite the varied verbal rhythms of each piece. The slight alterations necessary for respecting the science and art of this little melody in adapted form is applied with such integrity and skill as only to add at times greater grace and attraction to the model melody in its adapted form, where it shares its musical raiment with a sister text.

In order to better appreciate the qualities just proposed, it would be well to sing consecutively each of the pieces, giving heed to the details brought out in their analysis. Music, like any other art, cannot be perceived by statistical dissection alone. However, by the fact that it *can* be scrutinized in this manner and found more perfect than one might have judged through even long association with it, proves that it bears the stamp of *durability*, one of the characteristics of all genuine art.

Another of the most widely adapted melodies is that of the Antiphon 1) *Beáti pacífici* (1112), a song which Vincent d'Indy appraises as " a penetrating melody which follows all the rules of a good melody. " In adaptation of this Antiphon melody with that of 2) *Qui míhi* (1125) and *Qui vult* (1128), we look first for the relative number of syllables in the four melodic phrases of each piece : 1) 7, 7, 5, 5, versus 2) 6, 4, 6, 9, versus 3) 7, 7, 7, 5. The text of 1 comprises but three phrases but the melody concedes to a fourth, starting with the word *Déum*. In fact, prolongation of the preceding word, *ípsi* with a *distropha* arrived at in scale progression on its last syllable, shows plainly that the scribe felt a musical pause at this place. We shall therefore analyze this Antiphon on a four-phrase basis.

In the first phrase, the note D, tonic of Mode 1, is used for the initial tonic accent in both 1 and 2, as first note of the *clivis* D-C in 1 and in 2, and singly in 3. Both phrases in 1 and 2 contain but two verbal accents, as opposed to three in Antiphon 3. Had the latter, with one more verbal accent than in 1 and 2, used D for the first two of these accents, in order to accord only its last accent with F, as is done in 1 and 2, the note D would have appeared here four consecutive times, an unlikely procedure for any musician under the circumstances. Accordingly, two Fs are employed for these two final accented syllables, and in interesting setting, singly the first time and as first note of the *quilisma* F-G-*a* the second time.

In the second phrase all three Antiphons use *b♭* for the first tonic accent, singly in 1, as first note of the *clivis b♭-a* in 2 and 3. The final tonic accent is supported by the *podatus* F-*a* in the same phrase for each piece.

In phrase 3 the final tonic accent of the three chants is highlighted with *a*, dominant of Mode 1, used as first note of the *clivis a*-G in 1 and 3, singly in 2.

The two final verbal accents of phrase four, tonic in 1, rhythmic for *et* in 2 and 3, all use the same note, E : as first note of the *podatus* E-F in 1, singly in 2 and 3. For the four extra syllables in 2 new melodic material, actually a two-note sequence of the three preceding notes, is used for its first three syllables. From here on the notes remain the same in 1 and 2, with the *podatus* in 1 set as single notes in 2, because of one extra syllable in the latter. All three Antiphons use the modal tonic D for their final tonic accent, singly in 1 and 2, as the first note of the *podatus* D-F in 3. This neum is set in contrary movement to its two foregoing and following notes, that which accords particular grace to the cadence at this place.

A doctrinal sentiment prevails in these three evangelical texts, and it is enlightening to reflect that these ancient artisans of melody and word respected this characteristic in their subject matter to a degree of understanding that prompted them never to exploit their "originality" in the guise of musicianship nor for the sake of personal expression.

In the Style of Theme and Variation

A classic example in liturgical plainchant of theme and variation through inner development is found in the Antiphon *Váde Anania* (1343), the three phrases of whose theme proper produce a perfect ternary, or Lied, type of melody. The first phrase modulates to *d*, dominant of Mode 7, and the second to *c*, dominant of Plagal Mode 8.

A broad arsic movement soars upward from the start of the first phrase, then moves thetically downward from the beginning of the second phrase, continuing to the close of the third. The variations as a whole follow the same melodic line as the original theme.

Phrase 1 is varied in the first section after the full-stop; phrase two is varied in the next section, and phrase three in the final section. All three varied sections are effected with no notes other than the ones used in the original phrases.

At the start of the first variation, the major fifth G-*d*, preceded by a preparatory note, is innerly developed down to the close of the third variation, with the word *régibus*. The variations proper are actually completed at this point with the first note of the *clivis* G-F; but the added length of the text demands a coda. For the words *et filiis* new material is used. For the final word, *Israel*, the last five notes of the third phrase in the original theme are repeated, a strong cadence which is only enhanced through its repetition at the close of the variations. An added touch of artistry is the manner in which the final of the Psalm Tone moves in contrary movement to the intonation of the Antiphon.

This entire chant with its series of notes of passage, repetition, after-beats, etc., is comprised within the scope of the G-*e* hexachord. A good manner in which to appreciate this little chef-d'œuvre is to sing the three phrases of the original theme singly, following each immediately by its variation. This short Antiphon might well serve as model for developed works in the theme and variation category, if for nothing more than to be advised of the degree of perfection to which a monody of this type can arrive with but six diatonic notes.

Recall of Theme

The vigorous motif of the intonation " O " of the Advent Antiphons known by that name (340, ff.), is a perfect example of recall of the motif or theme at characteristic places, a procedure already examined in the *Te Déum*. The texts of the " O " Antiphons recall the promise of God to the Prophets that He would send the Messias.

In all seven of these Antiphons the initial interval of a fourth, C-F, is innerly developed during the course of the intonation proper. The same interval is repeated for the word *véni* in six of the Antiphons. In contrast to the " O " motif with its persistent *pressus*, which gives it the allure of impatient souls crying out with longing to the awaited Messias, the unadorned major fourth and easy half-step of the word *véni* lend a tender and humble appeal to this repeated cry that is quite different from the introductory " O. " Here again is seen an example of the modest procedures used by our early Church musicians for expressing varied emotions of such profound nature.

In six of the Antiphons the first note of the word *véni* is a repetition of the single note on the preceding syllable, C. The Antiphon *O Oriens* follows the same procedure of repetition, but because of the greater brevity of its text than that of the remaining six chants, the word *véni* arrives here one melodic phrase sooner than in the remaining pieces, which means that it starts with *a*, last note of the preceding *torculus*. In this loftier setting it emerges from the summit of the preceding melodic line topped with a double *torculus*, a climatic setting which accords it great dramatic flavor.

In the Antiphon *Hódie Chrístus nátus est* (413) the motif appears four times, as its each entrance consecutively heralds the advent of Christ in His Incarnation, His appearance in the world, the Song of the Angels, and the exultation of the Just.

The little motif on the first and third *hódie* is interspersed with a slightly modified one a degree lower, on the last two syllables of the word, a gentle transposition that lends tonal variety to the repeated word.

The simple melodic form of this motif is not sufficiently revealing to express the exultation of the Just who join the Angels in their song of rejoicing. Accordingly, on the final *hódie* the melody soars from *a*, dominant of Mode I, to *d*, summit of the Mode, on the beautiful composite neum that rounds off this thrice-repeated word, as men of good will unite with the citizens of heaven in their " Glória in excélsis Deo. "

In the canticle Antiphon of the Epiphany, *Tríbus miráculis* (466) the same procedure of tonal variety as that just described is used for slight variation between the three *hódie* motives. The rise of a fifth on the breve syllable of the first and third of these motives is interspersed by the rise of a fourth on the same syllable at its second entrance.

Immediately after exposition of the motif in each of these appearances, it is innerly developed during the course of its continued melodic phrase. In each phrase this development courses up and down in undulating arsic and thetic movements of singable intervals, as the text unfolds the story of the three manifestations of the Divinity of Christ : the Star that led the Magi to the Crib, the Water made Wine at the nuptial feast, the Baptism by John in the river Jordan. A lovely neumatic melody flows around the added words at the coda as they reveal the cause and effect of these miracles—in order that we may be saved.

Melodic Procedures for Dramatic and Symbolic Elements

Symbolic melodic and tonal representation of the sentiment of the text, a characteristic of all classical song, is portrayed as well in Gregorian Chant, in its own particular idiom. In the following Antiphon group we see first an example of this in the little piece *Púer Jésus* (437). This chant is an example of psalmodic form expressed with freedom. The calm and easy scope of Mode 6, "like a flower of the earth, expresses well the obscure and peaceful childhood of Jesus" (Gevaert). The upward scale movement on the melodic line of *proficiébat*, terminating with the energetic *podatus a-c* on the tonic accent of *aetáte*, manifests symbolically that Jesus *advanced* in age and in wisdom. The significant word *sapiéntia* is broadly asserted on its tonic and secondary accents, the latter with a *clivis*, the former with a *podatus*, in this otherwise quasi-syllabic chant, after which the breve and final syllables, the former decorated with a *clivis*, the latter with a lingering *distropha* and *pressus* as composite neum, accord appropriate importance to the word which reveals the summit of the Gifts of the Holy Spirit. The cadence of this Antiphon, C-F, is, as suggested by Willi Apel, a later modification in order to close the melody in Mode 6, whereas it originally closed on D, tonic of Mode I. [1] The form of the cadence as it now stands is a happy modification, in that these cadence notes are an inversion of the intonation, F-C.

In another sphere of thought we have the poetically expressed comparison of the Three Theological Virtues admirably symbolized melodically in the Antiphon *Máneant in vóbis* (663).

At the start, the admonishment "Máneant" stands out boldly on the G-C tetrachord in scale ascent. It then works downward in contrary movement, again in scale progression, to prepare for the lofty rise which starts with *fídes*, up through *spes* to the climatic word *cáritas* at the summit of the melodic line. The tonic accent of *cáritas* is forcefully asserted on *d*, dominant of Mode 7. When the text reaches this point there is no relaxation of the melody but rather reinforcement, for it repeats the three *torculus* -set notes on *cáritas* with the first three notes of the following word, *tría*. The melody then continues downward toward its modal tonic at the final of the fourth phrase. In this section, a melodic echo of the first phrase, the Apostle sets forth the hierarchy of the Three Theological Virtues, which "should remain in us."

[1] W. APEL, *op. cit.*, pp. 176, 266.

In rendition of this Antiphon a slight *mora vocis* should punctuate the words *fides* and *spes*, as is indicated for *cáritas*, just as this sequence would be uttered in well-delivered discourse.

An effective example of melodic symbolism occurs in the Antiphon *Ecce ascéndimus* (1086). As Christ announces to His disciples " Ecce ascéndimus " the melody rises steadily to the sixth degree of Mode 7, during which course the tonic accent of *ascéndimus* is strongly supported on *d*, dominant of the Mode. An arsic and thetic flow continues from here to the monosyllable *ad*. At this point, after the significant word *tradétur*, the melody takes an unexpected upward spring of a fourth to the strong tonal *podatus d-e*, a startling musical effect which brings to mind the full emotional import of that which the Savior suddenly remembers awaits Him at Jerusalem—Betrayal and Crucifixion.

A further example of melodic symbolism may be cited in the exquisite little Antiphon *Ecce ancílla Dómini* (1417). The intonation starts on *c*, dominant of Mode 8, a less usual procedure than use of a note closer to the modal tonic at this place in a chant piece. A happy exception is made in this song in order that the immortal words of the Handmaid of God as she *goes down* in humility befor her " Fiat " to become the Mother of the Redeemer, may be harmoniously symbolized in a parallel line, a comparison first made by Gevaert.

As contrast to the sentiment of the Antiphon just studied, the Church, in the diversity of the spirit, modulates also in songs of grandiose breadth such as the Antiphon *Vídi Dóminum* (995) and *Qui caelórum* (997), " whose prophetic texts are echoed in these two chants belonging to the noble Aeolian (Church 1) Mode " (Gevaert).

The element of modality is also brought into play at times to symbolize the sentiment of the text. In the Antiphon *Ecce nómen* (317), Gevaert points out the " purposeful modulation " from Mode 1 to Mode 8, starting from the word *vénit* through the word *longínque*, wherein the change of Mode signifies a change of place for the " name of the Lord. " These modulations in liturgical plainchant are never entered nor left in abrupt manner. The note which leads into the modulation, *a*, for the

49

word *vénit* is a repetition of the preceding note, even as the final note of the modulation proper, G, is repeated for the monosyllable *et* for re-entrance into the original Mode.

Dialogue Form

Certainly some of the most perfect dramas in history, little as well as big, are found in the New Testament. Among the most intimate ones we may choose from Christ's discourses with humanity, or even from the people's intercourse among themselves. In the latter vein we will look first at the Antiphon *Quem vidístis* (395), a naive little dialogue between the common people and the humble shepherds.

It might be relevant to hear first what Ricciotti has to say about Christ's first visitors in this world : " Shepherds like these had the very worst reputation among the Scribes and Pharisees, for since they led a nomadic life on the plains where water was not abundant, they were dirty, smelly, ignorant of all the prescriptions regarding the washing of hands, the choice of foods, etc. They were, besides, reputed to be thieves. But though this excluded them from the law courts of the Pharisees, these lowly shepherds enter the royal court of the newborn Son of David by invitation of the celestial courtiers of the Most High. "

The melody of the aforenamed Antiphon is as unpretentious as the actors of the little drama itself; it all moves in the span of the C-F tetrachord. The note F, dominant of Mode 2, which sets the little tune in motion, is also largely employed for the tonic accents of the words throughout the piece. The melody courses in little rises and falls of a sixfold ritornelle theme among eight phrases for both groups of singers : C-D-F-E-C-E-D. There is one substitution, in the fifth entrance, where the final note of the theme is changed from tonic D to dominant F. For from here the melody rises to a higher range as " the choir of Angels praise the Lord, allelúia, allelúia. "

The remarkable feature of this sixfold theme is that it never becomes monotonous, and this for two reasons : first, the varied rhythm of the words lends variety to the melody itself, and secondly, the actual charm of this diminutive chant is the short folk-song character of its melody. The singable " allelúias " with their flowing melody bring this little song, refreshing as a morning breeze, to a close.

The Antiphon *Fíli quid fecísti* (477) is a further gem in this dialogue series. The simple three-note intonation of a second expresses well the tenderness of the relieved Mother as she addresses her Son. Then, when she questions Him with a touch of delicate reproach, the melody rises in intensity and remains in an elevated range, as she relates to her Child the mental anguish she and His father suffered while sorrowing they sought Him. With the word *doléntes* the melody moves symbolically downward from G to D. The composite neum on the tonic accent of this word, wherein the first note of the *clivis* F-E is reinforced by its repetition on the first note of the following *climacus*, F-E-D, forcefully expresses the intensity of this sorrowing Mother. The melody then rises in scale intervals as the tonic accent of the meaningful word *quaerebámus* emerges on the strongly defined *podatus* G-*a*.

At this point the melody takes a sudden and unexpected upward spring from the tonic to the modal dominant for the dynamic word *Quid* on the tonally-accented *podatus c-d*, as the Child asks in a tone of surprise *how* it is that His parents sought Him. The melody continues in the high melodic range through the word *quaerebátis*, whose tonic accent echoes the *c-d podatus* of *Quid*. This strong neum is used for the third time on the tonic accent of the significant word *neciebátis*, which completes the element of surprise in the Son's query to His Mother.

The remainder of the song is clothed in calm syllabic chant of waving arsic and thetic line, as the Child reveals to His parents the reason for His remaining in the Temple without their knowledge : It was necessary that He be about His Father's business—the alpha and omega of His sojourn in this world.

Another little masterpiece in dialogue construction is the Antiphon *Dómine si tu vis* (491), short discourse between the Leper and the Master. The man of misery addresses the Divine Physician in the meekest and humblest of tones, symbolized

51

melodically by the little scale rise of a third on the vocative *Dómine*. Then, spurred on by the physical distress of his condition, his timidity diminishes as he continues to tell the Lord that if He *will* He can make him *clean*. The climatic word *vis* is melodically emphasized by a composite neum in contrary movement.

The following phrase is a further example of harmonious play. Here the arsic notes of the consecutive tonic accents of the words move down in scale fashion to a modal note of rest, each note of the first two tonic accents interspersed with an " after-beat " note one degree higher than the tonic accent note itself.

At the close of the next phrase the atonic syllable of the word *Jésus* modulates supplely on a double *torculus*, rounded off on the modal dominant *a* in order to prepare the entrance of this note singly on the tonic accent of *Vólo*, the most powerful word in the text. Had the tonic accent of this word been accompanied by even a two-note neum, the power of this declamation would have been lessened. As it is, the *climacus* on its atonic syllable, sliding down in scale intervals from the *punctum*, broadens the word sufficiently, and at the same time leads smoothly into the liquescent *torculus* of the word *mundáre*. The melodic repetition, with slight mutation, of this latter word in its second appearance, now as an imperative, would seem to indicate that Jesus echoed it with the element of urgency with which it was spoken by the leper whom He cured.

If we picture to ourselves the tremendous import of these scenes, I daresay we will not remain melodically and dramatically insensitive to their significance.

Surely one of the most appealing situations in the Gospels is that of the persecuted woman taken in adultery by her pharisaic accusers and brought before the Man who was to become her advocate. This affecting scene is depicted in the Antiphon *Némo te condemnávit* (558), which we have already studied in its melodic quatenary form. This piece is a little drama in four acts : question, answer, response, exhortation.

Christ addresses the distressed woman quietly in order not to add to her fright. Thus the melody opens with the simple Psalm Tone 3 intonation and remains on the dominant of the Mode, *c*, as anticipation for the *clivis c-d* on the tonic accent of the salient word *condemnávit*. There is certainly no harshness in utterance of the word *múlier*, with flexible undulating neums entwined around its syllables.

The very tone of the Savior as much as His regard of pity must have lent a certain reassurance to the victim, for her answer is accompanied by a melodic figure that starts on the dominant *c*, four degrees higher than the last note of the previous phrase. With the word *Némo* we have a further example (as in *Vólo*) of the tonic accent of a virile assertive word strongly emphasized with but a single note. In this case the two-note neum on the atonic syllable likewise broadens the word proportionately.

In the third phrase the Lord's response starts on the last note of the woman's answer, *b*, original dominant of Mode 3. Apparently loud enough in this high melodic range for the self-righteous accusers all to hear, the Lord disclaims added judgment on His part of the already cruelly judged woman. The tonic accent of the decisive word *condemnábo*, preceded by its negative *nec*, is highlighted, as it was in the past tense; this time with a forceful *scandicus* to the modal dominant.

In the last act of this little drama, the exhortation, the word *ámplius* rises to the seventh degree of the Mode, *d*, then descends to prepare for the graver part of the utterance : *nóli peccáre*. The first note of each *podatus* in the melody of these words, together with the final verbal tonic accent note, produces the harmonious cadence, F-G-E, as this soul-stirring scene comes to an end.

Conclusion

In analysis of these so simple appearing songs one discovers the amount and degree of reflection that must have been put into the composition or adaptation, as the case may be, of each melody, in order that it might serve as a worthy associate of the inspired text. Accordingly, a survey of the Antiphons even

53

as limited as this one shows how inapt it would be to sing all the chant pieces in identical interpretive manner, in paying more heed to less important factors than to the characteristics of each individual song. Of course technical precision should be present in any finished product of art, but, at the same time, one should not lose sight of the *expressive* element, which, in the last analysis, is the final and whole-comprising stamp of all creation, of whatever product it may be.

It is quite conceivable that certain eminent musicologists do not accept the thesis of " expression " in its over-all concept for Gregorian Chant. Certainly all liturgical plainchant does not embody the melodic symbolism that the texts portray. In fact, some melodic lines do just the contrary. However, there would seem to be sufficient evidence in the Gregorian repertory to substantiate the claim that a marked degree of modal and melodic play which corresponds to dramatic and expressive elements is not the result of accident.

In order to be consistent, we must keep ever before our eyes that not only is the expressive element of liturgical plainchant in another sphere than that of our modern epoch of music, but also that the modest amount of melodic material at the disposition of the chant composers would in itself preclude anything other than the simplest procedures for portraying dramatic and symbolic elements in their particular orbit of action.

In addition, it would seem no more reasonable to interpret two chant pieces of dissimilar text sentiment and melodic construction in like interpretive rendition than it would be to do the same for a Beethoven Andante and a Beethoven Scherzo, both in the same sonata or symphony. To be sure the drama of liturgical plainsong is not that of a Wagnerian opera nor even that of the Lieder of Schubert, Schumann and Brahms, but it *is* that of Holy Scripture, wherein is found drama of the highest degree. The impassioned expression in no way finds place in this liturgically spiritual song; however, there is vast difference between this type of interpretation governed by " feeling, " legitimate as it may be in its particular sphere, and one nourished by a perception that visualizes interiorly

54

the character of the work and manifests this sentiment with the technical equipment at one's command.

Can we imagine Christ's having uttered His doctrine in the same tone of voice and with the same intensity at all times? If we are looking for contrast let us take two situations, such as the castigation of hypocrites and the Sermon on the Mount. Consider likewise the innumerable varied sentiments of the utterances of the Prophets and the songs of the Psalmists expressed in their delivery of the same, and which texts comprise the bulk of the Divine Liturgy.

The integrity of particular composition, hence interpretation, for individual chants in the sung liturgy is borne out in classical treatises of the Middle Ages. The author of *Musica Enchiriades* of the ninth century [1] shows how " the peaceful motives are used for tranquil things, joyful motives for pleasant ones, sad motives for grievous ones; that which is said or done with hardiness is expressed in lively motives, with suddeness, vehemence, emotion, and the other qualities that describe events and dispositions, so that in this way the motives and the words are determined as *one* in the smallest particulars. Because of these procedures we are able to search out the meanings, notwithstanding the fact that much is hidden to us beneath occult matter. Thus in this way we relish the gifts of God, praising Him in like degree, and those things which we discovered with the old laborious investigations are received in jubilation, celebration, song; things which were not made known in former generations to the sons of men, but are now revealed to His saints. "

A century later, a treatise attributed to St. Odo of Cluny (*idem,* 276), supports this judgment of particular interpretation in accordance with the varied sentiments which reign in the diverse liturgical chants, and which are distinguishable through the authoritative and reasoning qualities of the music. The writer continues by asserting that we are imbued " not with the science of the flesh, but with that of the spirit, with confidence,

---

[1] GERBERT, *Scriptores Ecclesiastici,* I, p. 172.

55

so that proceeding quickly to knowledge of these works of art, we likewise understand them and pursue them, and we perceive in the words that which is satisfactorily expressed with the letters of the music. "

These sound doctrines of our first musicologists would seem to lend strong evidence to the thesis that the songs of liturgical plainchant, nucleus of Occidental dramatic music, contain within themselves characteristics of expressive interpretation.

In speaking of the particular procedures followed by our ancient composers as a means of more forcefully portraying the meaning of the text, a modern liturgical musician has written the following : " All that is not the fruit of chance, but of a very conscious will with the composer to put in special relief the ideas which were close to his heart. One must put himself at *their* school and learn to read *their* thoughts not only through the sometimes subtle and yet very naive arrangement of the text, but particularly through the light of musical expression which this gives the texts and which can certainly, if we know how to understand it, make us penetrate further into the traditional theology of the Church. " [1]

In liturgical song there is lightness (as in the delightful little Antiphon of the shepherds and the people) as well as gravity, joy as well as sorrow, jubilation as well as fear, calm as well as emotion. Should we remain impassive before this God-given variety of sentiment, in timid restraint, for fear of appearing " subjective ? " If we view the matter objectively we will give little heed to any such affectations, but rather substitute for them the wholesome recognition due the rightful claims of a supernatural art that still retains—and just because it *is* of supernatural origin—the diverse sentiments with which it is divinely endowed.

The Apostle justifies this procedure in one of his inspired admonishments : " Therefore let him who speaks in a tongue pray that he may *interpret*. For if I pray in a tongue my spirit

[1] Dom M. A. RIVIÈRE, O.S.B., *L'Église qui chante* (1957).

prays, but my *understanding* is unfruitful. What, then, is to be done? I will pray with the spirit, but *I will pray with the understanding also;* I will sing with the spirit, but *I will sing with the understanding also.* Else if thou givest praise with the spirit alone, how shall he who fills the place of the uninstructed say ' Amen ' to thy thanksgiving? For he does not know what thou sayest. For thou, indeed, givest thanks well, but the other is not edified. I thank God that I speak with all your tongues; yet *in the church I had rather speak five words with my understanding, that I may also instruct others, than ten thousand words in a tongue. ''* (I Cor 14, 13-20.)

PART THREE

PROPER OF THE MASS

INTROIT

History

The Eucharistic Sacrifice comprises three processions : 1) The entrance of the Pontiff into the church, Introit; 2) The procession of the faithful carrying their offerings for sacrifice, Offertory; 3) The communicants going to the Eucharistic Banquet, Communion. The chants which accompanied these processions appeared nearly at the same time as the processions themselves.

The Introit and Communion can be traced back to the fifth century, and both developed in like manner. They had their origin in antiphonal singing of a Psalm at the beginning and end of Mass. According to the *Liber Pontificalis* (6th c.) St. Celestine (d. 432) was the first Pope to prescribe alternating chanting *(psalli antephonatum)* of all the Psalter before Mass. However, the thought of the Pontiff must have been that the 150 Psalms were to be distributed between the Sundays and feast days throughout the year.

An entire Psalm, or at least series of verses of a Psalm, were sung by the congregation at the entrance *(introitus)* of the Pontiff into the church. According to a ninth century ordo, the Psalm started as the celebrant and assistants left the sacristy at the side of the principal entrance into the church, and terminated with the *Glória Pátri* at a sign from the Pontiff after his arrival at the altar.

At Rome the singing of the Introit was taken by the *schola* at an early age. By the time of St. Gregory it was already a developed chant. The first Roman ordo (c. 770) describes it as a chant of the *schola*, but in Gaul there is evidence of participation of the faithful in rendition of the Introit until the ninth century, although their part in it may have been reduced to that of the doxology alone. Charlemagne ordained that the " *Glória Pátri* should be sung by *all* with reverence. "

Form

The Introit acts as a " herald " for the sentiment of the feast which the Mass celebrates. As the preliminary ceremonies of the Mass became shortened the number of Psalm verses was cut down. Although certain later manuscripts still retain the early form, by the ninth and tenth centuries the Introit was reduced to its present form, as given in the eleventh century Roman ordo : Antiphon, Psalm verse, *Glória Pátri* (with *Sícut érat*), and a closing repetition of the Antiphon : A-B-C-A. The first verse is marked *Ps.*, remnant of its origin as a Psalm.

Peter Wagner states that the rule that the texts were taken from the Psalms or other parts of the Bible cannot be laid down as universally true, and he continues in stating that " the Introits of the oldest feasts of Our Lord have their texts taken by preference from the historical and other books. Before the time of Pope Celestine the Introit Antiphon was seldom taken from the Psalms. The later Masses as well as those of the *Sanctorale* have their texts taken from the Psalms, because in them might be found the glorification of every Christian virtue. Moreover, the Psalter was from the beginning the chant book of the Church, so that it was always drawn upon for Masses of no special significance. The Psalter has been especially employed for the Introits of Lent and the Sundays after Pentecost. "[1] In the original nucleus the Introit texts preserve the mounting order of the Psalter, starting with Psalm 12, 17, 24, etc.

In the category of chant pieces constructed upon the form of psalmody, three types of melody prevail in general lines : 1) Simple in character, as the Psalms of the Office; 2) Ornate, as the Introit and Communion of the Mass; 3) Melismatic,

---

[1] Peter WAGNER, *Einführung in die Gregorianischen Melodien* (Berlin : Breilkopf & Hartel, 1911), I, pp. 69, 70.

or florid, as the Gradual, Alleluia, and Offertory of the Mass. The difference in the style of these three groups is purely accidental. All are built on the structure of pure psalmody : intonation, dominant, mediant cadence (often preceded by one or more temporary cadences), return to the dominant (often two or more temporary cadences), final cadence. The development in the ornate and neumatic style is not a thematic one through engendering of new themes; it is simply variety in the same theme. The Propers composed after Pentecost are later than those of the other seasons or cycles. They are also more ornamental.

As stated, the Introit is but a moderately melismatic chant. For the Psalm verse and doxology particular melodies are fashioned for each of the eight Psalm Tones, in the style of the ornate psalmody of the Canticles. However, unlike the Solemn Tone Canticle melodies, wherein only the mediant cadence is ornamented while the final remains the same as the corresponding Psalm Tone, in the ornamental Tones of the Introit both cadences are melodically effected. Tones I, IV, V, VI, VIII have a choice between two final cadences. Tones II, III and VII have but one final cadence.

The finals of the Introit Tones, as in the case of the finals of the Office Antiphons and their corresponding Psalm Tones, are likewise fashioned to lead smoothly into the particular intonation of the Introit Antiphon to which they are allied, even as the cadences of the latter are devised to do the same in leading into the intonation of the Introit Tone. As Dom Pothier asserts : " At every page of the Gradual and Antiphonary is seen the same care to harmonize all according to the most delicate rules of taste, in the manner that not only every phrase taken by itself flows with that naturalness and clarity that are ever the stamp of works that are both natural and beautiful, but that moreover ever flow and unite with one another with freedom and calm. "

The Introit *Gaudeámus* (1368), one of the most frequently adapted melodies, serves as an example of psalmodic form. This chant was composed originally for the Feast of St. Agatha.

It has a parallel in the Milanese Ingressa *Laetámur*. Its text may be a translation from the Greek Office. St. Agatha is a Sicilian, and in the southern territories there existed many Greek rites even to the ninth and tenth centuries. Peter Wagner includes also the Introits *Sálus pópuli* (1059) and *Dícit Dóminus : Sermónes* (1758) as translations from the Greek.

Gaudeámus has the same *incipit* (opening motif) often found in Antiphons of Mode 1, an intonation already described: C-D-*a-b♭-a*. Here the modal dominant is established. As the melody progresses, three suspensive cadences follow in order, ending consecutively on *a*, dominant of Mode 1, F, mediant, and *a*. At this point the song arrives at the mediant cadence with a full-stop. The ensuing melodic course likewise comprises three suspensive cadences, ending in turn on G, F, G, subdominant, mediant, subdominant. Then follows a final cadence which closes on the modal tonic D.

It is easy to see in what beautiful proportion this melody is formed, with its like number of cadences in each of the two parts, the balance of verbal and melodic thought divided at the mediant. The same harmonious proportion exists between the intonation and final cadence, two motives which complement one another, the first of which puts the melodic march in motion, the second which brings it to rest.

Tonality

All eight Modes are represented in the Introits. *Exsúrge* (504) is a typical example of Mode 1, an Introit which Dom Ferretti appraises as " a masterpiece of Gregorian Chant. " There is no *b♭* (the " accidental note ") during the course of its melody.

At times there is disagreement among chant specialists regarding the appropriation of a certain Mode to a particular piece. For example, Dom Dominic Johner considers the Introit *Spíritus Dómini super me* (1579) as belonging to Mode 8 rather than to Mode 3. As previously stated in tonal study of the Antiphon, both Modes have the same dominant, *c*. Furthermore, they frequently use like procedures for melodic treatment.

In developed chant pieces there is often mixture of an

Authentic with its Plagal Mode, or vice versa. In the Introit *Víri Galilaéi* (846), intermingling of the closing cadences on G and *c*, tonic and dominant of Mode 8, from the close of the intonation through *véniet*, produce the tonality of the latter Mode intermingled with its Authentic Mode 7. The intermingling of Authentic and Plagal Modes in the same piece was called *mixtus* by medieval theorists. A scale can transcend the octave, called *superabundans* by the medieval theorists, but not beyond a degree, otherwise it would be considered in its allied Mode, unless it modulates into another scale.

At other times different Modes appear in the same piece. The Introit *Reminíscere* (545) may certainly be considered in Mode 2 rather than in Mode 4 from the initial note, D, tonic of Mode 2, on through the word *unquam*. During the course of the melody to this point, F, dominant of Mode 2, is projected with a *tristropha* at the start of four different melodic phrases alone, and in addition is used as closing note for five of the six short cadences in this melodic course. This section comprises a little over half of the Antiphon proper. The anguished *líbera nos* is all the more effective not only because of its rising melody on *líbera*, but also because with this cry the modulation into Mode 4 is established. The same dominant play of F in Mode 4 occurs in the Easter Introit, *Resurréxi* (778). See also the Introit *Misericórdia* (816) and *In voluntáte* (1066) for like modal procedure.

A piece may remain in the same Mode and at the same time employ transposition of one or more of its motives. In the Introit *Miseréris ómnium* (525) the word *paeniténtiam* is accompanied by a motif in the tonality of *a*, dominant of Mode 1. This motif occurs a second time on the atonic syllable of *Déus* through *nóster*, in the tonality of D, tonic of the Mode.

The virile character of the dominant of the Mode is often employed as theoretic procedure for stressing the important words of the text. In the Introit *Gaudeámus*, which we have already seen in the section on form, the same motif is used for the three significant words, *honóre*, *passióne*, and *caulláudant*. In each of these words the *torculus* or the *podatus* with its energetic spring of a third from the modal dominant *a*, preceded by a lower appoggiatura note, G, provides a support of such satisfying vigor for the tonic accent of each of these words, that it appears to have been so perfectly suited for the purpose of emphasis as to have been chosen three times for that intention. Especially in this piece does it gain in significance as used for the particular words which together incorporate the sentiment of the text.

As for laying undue stress on the designation of a particular Mode in relation to the song, Dom Pothier has this to say: " The Gregorian melodies may be named and classified according as you will, but they lose none of their value. It is with them as with the flowers of the garden. Botanists describe and classify them in various ways, but each retains the beauty and form with which divine art endowed it, and the natural odor of the honey, which the bees, more wise and intelligent than our sages, are able to extract. "

Adaptation

The Mass of the Holy Trinity is probably the first occasion on which pre-existing Mass melodies were adapted to new texts, a feast for which Alcuin (d. 814) wrote the text. Rome did not insert Trinity Sunday into its calendar until the fourteenth century.

Textual phrase dissimilarities between original verbal texts and adapted ones will often oblige that certain readjustments of melodic phrase endings be effected. For example, in the case of adaptation of the Introit *Invocábit me* (532), of the first Sunday of Lent, to the text of the Trinity Sunday Introit, *Benedícta sit* (909), the first and fourteen-syllable textual phrase of the original setting closes with the word *éum*. In the adapted version the first and ten—syllable textual phrase closes with the word *Trínitas*, a condition which brings its melodic phrase to a close the length of two neums before that of the original version. Notwithstanding, the phrase ending on the modal dominant *c* in the adapted setting is sufficiently satisfying for a place of temporary pause, and particularly because of the textual division after *Trínitas*, although it must be admitted that the neum which takes off from this place without pause in the original version unquestionably brings the phrase to a more fully complete cadence on the modal tonic G.

It is interesting to see the ingenuity displayed in like melodic setting of these two verbal texts of pronounced rhythmic dissimilarity, which we will look at in these two Masses.

The tonic accent of the initial word in each piece, 1) *Invocábit me,* 2) *Benedícta sit,* is strongly asserted with the *torculus resupinus.* The *tristropha c,* dominant of Mode 8, on the tonic accent of *exáudium* in 1 finds its counterpart (with slight rhythmic change) on the tonic accent of the word *Trínitas* in 2. The same neums are employed for the remaining verbal accents with the curtailed ending already pointed out in 2. From *erípiam* in 1 and *divísa* in 2 to the close of *éum* in 1 and *Unitas* in 2, the neums which accompany the first verbal accents in each are the same, with no change of melody in 2, despite the variant verbal rhythms in each version. A saliant neum with the upper spring of a fourth, from the tonic to the dominant of the Mode, is reserved for the tonic accent of the significant word *erípiam* in 1. The adapter has done the same for the equally significant word *indivísa* in 2.

The very beautiful melisma on the words *glorificábo éum* in 1, with its series of undulating neums in contrary movement rising a degree beyond the summit of the Mode on the tonic accent of *glorificábo,* is mirrored for the words of diverse rhythm, *confitébimur éi* in 2, a verbal counterpoint of profound significance—God's glorification of man versus man's glorification of God. In the rhythmically diverse words *longitúdine diérum* of 1 and *quia fécit nóbis* of 2, the adapter has varied the melody as little as possible. The dynamic note *d,* which demands resolution, is used for the tonic accent of *longitúdinem* in 1 and for *fécit* of 2, with the same repeated flowing cadence for the last word of the same phrase in each piece. But here is a case where the adapter has faithfully followed the melodic phrasing of the original version to the sacrifice of the textual division of 2, wherein *cum* should be united to *misericórdiam.*

65

At *ad implébo* of the final phrase of 1, the original version employs a melody of classic type which rises and falls in true vocal art. The adapter has skillfully applied it to the longer and rhythmically diverse word *misericórdiam* in 2. The repeated cadence of this vocalization in both versions brings to a close a work of worthy adaptation. Notwithstanding diverse rhythmic texts, the song writer has retained the original melody with the least possible mutation in its adapted form. Furthermore, where possible, a strong modal note or rhythmic neum has been retained from the original setting of tonic accents, for application to tonic accents in adaptation of the original melody to a variant text.

The foregoing adaptation is obviously a product of the so-called " Silver Age. " And here a word of recognition for this most difficult of tasks would not seem to be irrelevant.

It is evidently impossible to adapt the melody of a verbal text of individual phrasing and syllable number to the melody of an original verbal text of dissimilar phrasing and syllable number, without resorting to certain mutations in the adapted version. Two absolutely identical settings can never be effected unless both texts are identical in the form and length of their phrases and the number of their syllables. Since this condition is so rare as to be generally nonexistent, the most important task that remains is to endeavor to employ the original matter in the contrary condition with least injury to the verbal and melodic demands of each version.

It bears repetition to say that study of this most exigent of tasks affords an opportunity to see that, despite the impossibility of arriving at an entirely perfect product of work, because of the conditions, it is evident that the early adapters carefully weighed the textual and melodic potentialities of these sacred songs before setting their work down on parchment. Melodic adaptation to various verbal texts is a labor rarely encountered in posterior epochs of music. It obviously demands a particular endowment of talent, bestowed light, and incalculable patience for its accomplishment.

A further adaptation, also of a later epoch, is that of the Introit 1) *Ecce advénit* (459) to the Introit 2) *Sálve sáncta Párens* (1263). According to the *Liber Pontificalis* the Introit *Ecce advénit* is a translation from the Greek. *Sálve sáncta Párens* appears in manuscripts from the twelfth century on. Its hexameter verses are extracts from *Opus páschale* of Sedulius (c. 450).

The tonic accent of the initial salutation in each piece is accompanied by a forceful composite neum, starting on the lowest note of the second modal scale, A. In the second small phrase in each text, the tonic accent of the important words *advénit* in 1 and of *Párens* in 2, is supported by a like *quilisma* in the form of a *scandicus resupinus*. The text of the phrase which precedes the full-stop in both songs contains seven syllables in 1 and nine in 2. The adapter skillfully takes care of this diversity by adapting to the longer text a *podatus* as double appoggiatura to the first syllable of *eníxa* in 2, and a *pressus* to its tonic accent before entering into the series of four single notes at this place in 1. The extended repetition of these latter notes for the longer text in 2 would have been redundant. Fine taste is displayed in not giving the *distropha* to the tonic accent of *dominátor* in 1. Had this been done, with the natural prominence of the tonic accent as it is, rising a fourth to the modal dominant, it would have been disproportionately prolonged for syllabic chant. The ornamental cadence of this phrase is the same in both pieces.

From here on, to the full-stop in 1 and through *régit* of 2, the notes and their groupings are identical in both songs. At *régnum* of 1 and *caélum* of 2, we again see a case where a single note is applied to the tonic accent, with a *tristropha* reserved for the atonic syllable. The aesthetic principle for this has just been explained. In the same phrase a forceful *pressus* on the dominant of the Mode, F, is employed for the tonic accent of *mánu* in 1 and of *terrámque* in 2.

The mighty words *potéstas* in 1 and *saécula* in 2 have received a more virile setting through their melodic simplicity than if they had been melismatically decorated. Relatively important neums, a *distropha* and a *podatus*, are used respectively for the preparatory and tonic syllables of *potéstas* in 1, and for the tonic and breve syllable of *saécula* in 2. The motif used for these words is innerly developed in the concluding phrase of each song. Here the notes are the same in both pieces but the verbal rhythms are diverse. Notwithstanding, the tonic accents in each text are respected with melodic perfection, while at the same time the remaining syllables receive their proportionate ornamentation. Herein we find an entire adaptation free of either melodic or textual sacrifice.

While still on the subject of adaptation it is interesting to observe the settings of the same verbal text for two dissimilar pieces : the Antiphon of the Introit *Hódie scitis* (359) and the Gradual Respond of the same Mass (360), whose melody we shall treat more fully later in this study. Each piece with its traditional melodic style and form retains like conservation of verbal accentuation importance, with due proportion of the melody as a whole.

In even limited analytic work of this type one sees at close range the cautious manner with which these ancient musicians avoided the smallest unnecessary mutation of an original melody in its adaptation. When they had to insert or retract a note from the original version in setting it to a varied text, it is evident that they deliberated at length in order not only to conserve the original melody intact as far as possible, but what is equally, if not more, important, to respect the rhythmic verbal and melodic elements and the particular sentiment of the new text. They were manifestly imbued with the characteristic of these liturgical chants as dramatic music, songs in which the *words* as textual sentiment act as generator of the sung melody.

Centonization

We have seen that centonization occurs most frequently in the Graduals, Tracts and Responsories of Matins, as well as among the Office Antiphons to a certain degree. However, the *texts* of other liturgical pieces are frequently a product of centonization. For example, the text of the Introit *Pópulus Síon* (327) is extracted from various parts of the Book of Isaiah : 30 : 19, 29, 30; 40 : 10. The Introit *Fáctum est cor méum* (1477) is made up of extracts from Psalm 21 : 15 and 68 : 10. As for what Willi Apel calls " migrating phrases " (phrases transferred from one chant to another) this same author indicates but one example in the Introits : *Quasimódo* (809) and *Cantáte Dómino* (826), which have the same melody for " allelúia : rationábiles, sine dólo " and " allelúia : quia mirabília fécit Dóminus. " [1]

Melodic Procedures for Expressive and Symbolic Elements

As the Church cycle unfolds, the liturgical texts change in keeping with the sentiment of the season or feast. Accordingly, their allied melodies submit to appropriate symbolic or expressive change in keeping with the varied texts.

The spirit of hope for the advent of the Redeemer is symbolized in the Introit *Ad te levávi* (318). After the first dip of a fourth on the opening monosyllable, from the tonic of Mode 8, G, the melody ascends steadily with the rising expectation which the words of the text portray. The interval rise of a fourth on the tonic accent of *ánimam* and of a third on the tonic accent of *Déus*, at the outset of their respective phrases, claim an energetic impulse that carries the voice along to the close of each of their following cadences. The tonic accent of the key-word *confído*, ornamented with an elevated composite neum in contrary movement, symbolizes the Hebrew psalmist's spirit of confidence for Israel, even as the descending ornamental motif on *erubéscam* portrays the gravity of her perplexity, both sentiments applied to the Church for the Advent spirit of hope and penance.

The four-note dominant *c*, as prolonged *virga* and *tristropha* on the ultimate syllable of the strong negative *neque*, gives the impression of the tenacious assurance of a soul whose " neither " is a cry of unswerving faith in a divine power against the torments of its enemies. The tonic accent of the word *inimíci* rises

[1] *Op. cit.*, p. 311.

69

dramatically on a *quilisma*, lending emotion to the expressive pleading of the text. The melodic cadence on *confundántur*, at the final of the Antiphon, is an artistic variant of the one on *erubéscam* at the mediant of the song.

The liturgy enters next into celebration of the Incarnation. The three Christmas Masses are original; their melodies have no preceding duplication in the liturgy. Even their respective Modes reflect the sentiment of the text in each song. Dom Gregory Huegle calls the Midnight Mass Introit *Dóminus díxit* (392) a little lullaby sung by the Child to His Father. The gentle swaying of the *oriscus* on both syllables of the word *díxit* as well as on the tonic accent of *hódie*, is most conducive to this thought. The motif which follows the mediant cadence of the song, at *égo*, continuing through the first syllable of *hódie*, is an echo of the intonation motif on *Dóminus*, both being the same Person. The most ornate, but still modest, motif in the chant is reserved for the final cadence on the words which embody the mystery revealed in the text—*génui te*.

This little gem of a song is composed within the scope of the C-G pentachord. It would be difficult to know how a more appropriate melody could have been fashioned for the text of the greatest of mysteries told in miniature.

In contrast to the foregoing Introit, *Púer nátus est* of the third Christmas Mass (408), in the full light of day, rings out like a herald's trumpet. The bold rise of an unprepared fifth on *Púer* and its remaining motif on *nátus est*, is melodically echoed with slight mutation at *et fílius*. In this procedure the song writer not only draws attention to the identity of *Púer* and *fílius*, but at the same time makes sure that the heralding motif is heard by all through repetition. After its second appearance the fifth is innerly developed during the course of the remaining phrase.

The tonic accent of the majestic word *impérium*, which reveals the kingship of the Child, soars up on a double *podatus* to *f*, seventh note of modal scale 7. The melody on the words *húmerum éjus*, seven variant descending neums interspersed with a *tristropha*, is a little model of free-rhythm melody beautifully proportioned. This lofty text which reveals the Godhead of the little Child, is brought to a close with a strong cadence on the final word, *Angelus*.

In the majority of pieces in the Gregorian Chant repertory procedures of fine melodic workmanship are displayed for preserving the expressive sentiment of the text. Continuing with the Introit group, we observe that *Etenim sedérunt* (414) for Stephen's martyrdom, appropriately uses a melody of low melodic range for the word *persecúti*. The repeated D-F interval on the secondary and tonic accents of this word, the latter accent dynamically projected on three combined neums in contrary movement, gives emphatic portrayal to the *persistence* with which the wicked harass their victim. The motif on the words *in túis* is a skillful and conclusive variant of the one on the last two syllables of *exercebátur*. Let any composer try to write an interesting seven-note motif made up of but four diatonic tones and then variate it artistically with the same material, and he will begin to appreciate the unique ability possessed by these writers of song.

As each phase in the life of Christ enters into the scene of action, the sentiment of the Church's official liturgy and chant change accordingly. The Introit which opens the Season of Septuagesima, *Circumdedérunt me* (497), is a decided contrast to the buoyant *Púer nátus est* of the Birth of Christ. With *Circumdedérunt* the Church is starting to relive the Passion and Death of her Head, expressed in the anguished cry of the psalmist. The intonation remains in the lowest range of Mode 5, rising but a third; but with the urge of distress revealed in the text, the melody mounts with *gémitus*, up through *dolóres*, then descends symbolically for *inférni*, whose motif in turn leads into the superb ornamentation of the word *circumdedérunt* in its second appearance. This beautiful rolling melody which weaves around the syllables of the word, actually visualizes that which the term expresses.

At *tribulatióne* the melody returns symbolically to the lower span with recall of the intonation; but as the psalmist raises his voice to the Lord, the composer elevates the melody on *invocávi Dóminum*, its turbulent character augmented with a *salicus* (probably a later neum modification) at the peak of the melody, on the tonic accent of *invocávi*. The melody remains in a high range through *exaudívit* and that which follows, descending only for the cadence at *súo*. This leads smoothly into the rising ornamental motif on *vócem*, rounded off on its atonic syllable with a graceful *torculus*. Then follows a calm cadence. The melody thus lends added assurance to the text that God *heard* the anguished soul as it raised its voice in supplication.

In the Introit *Exsúrge* (504), already pointed out in the section on tonality, the psalmist cries out to the Lord in a tone of reproach for His apparent abandonment of Israel under oppression of military defeat. The Church applies this situation to Christ in His likewise apparent defeat at the hands of His enemies. Like the intonation of *Circumdedérunt*, the word *Exsúrge* also starts in the lowest range of its Mode, 1, rising but a third. But in case the Lord has not heard the first time, the psalmist cries out a second *exsúrge*, this time with greater intensity. The melody portrays this element of persistence not only through an elevated motif, but also with the aid of an energetic *pressus* and an added *podatus* on the tonic accent of *exsúrge*. The song writer uses a similar procedure of added melodic intensity for the repeated *quáre*, as the harassed soul persists in its " why " until it is heard and the Lord ceases to turn His face away from His chosen people in their hour of tribulation. The motif of the word *tribulatiónem*, a salient *salicus* on its tonic syllable, preceded by a repeated *podatus* on the secondary accent and its following syllable, lend satisfying melodic imploration to the sentiment of affliction incorporated in this word.

The melody remains in the same range until the atonic syllable of the word *térra*, where it drops appropriately downward, a fourth, to depict Israel's " belly cleaving to the earth. " When for the third time the psalmist calls out to the Lord to " rise, " the melody again moves upward, with a strong *podatus* given to the tonic accent of the twice-repeated " exsúrge. " The melody remains on the dominant of the Mode, *a*, for the tonic accent of *Dómine* and the vital outcry " ádjuva. " The key-words of the text, " líbera nos, " reserved for the cadence of the song, are ornamented with the breadth of a *salicus* on the tonic accent of *líbera*, proportioned by an undulating composite neum on its atonic syllable, which, with the final *clivis* on *nos* produces a perfect little arsic and thetic wave.

A further liturgical masterpiece of the Passion is the Introit *Júdica me* of Passion Sunday (569), whose text had already been used for this Introit before it was incorporated into the start of the Mass. This Introit also starts on the lowest note of the Mode, E. However, it remains but briefly in the lowest modal register, for the psalmist soon turns his eyes heavenward toward the source of his help, *Déus*. With this word the melody moves symbolically upward. It then descends to prepare for the lofty sudden soar to a *distropha* on *c*, a degree higher than the summit of the modal scale, on the tonic accent of the first of the significant words *cáusam méam*. This note is the later established dominant of Mode 3, into which the tonality now enters, and remains until the last phrase of the song.

The developed motives on the tonic accents of the dire words *hómine iníquo* and *dolóso* are wonderfully graded for revealing the fullness of dread which they express. The climax of the psalmist's cry, " erípe me, " the final words of supplication, receive a developed melodic treatment proportioned to the preceding words, and express the horror from which the distressed soul would be delivered. The strong *distropha* on the original dominant of Mode 3, *b*, used for the tonic accent of *erípe*, is in no way overshadowed by the ornamental neum on its atonic syllable, not only because of the strong modal note for the *distropha*, but also because the ornamental composite neum serves essentially as a proportionate intermediary between the three preceding notes and the two broadened ones at the feminine ending of the word.

From *quia* on the melody calms down, for the psalmist is now assured that his help is from Him who is both God and his strength. A motif of appropriate breadth is reserved for

73

fortitúdo, conducting this dramatic text with its final *méa* to a close.

The melody of the Introit of Psalm Sunday, *Dómine ne lónge* (590), extract from one of the most important of the Messianic Psalms (21 : 20, 22), highlights the climactic word *áspice*, projected in the most superior range of the song, rising abruptly a fourth from the preceding neum into the Authentic Mode 7 on the tonic accent of the word. The supplicating *líbera me* which follows remains in the upper register of Mode 8, melodic symbol of the psalmist's anguished cry as he calls on the Lord to deliver him from the mouth of the lion.

After the Resurrection, the liturgy, in contrasting mood to the foregoing Passiontide Introits, presents the joyful *Jubiláte Déo* of the Easter Season (821). The song remains throughout in the superior plane of Mode 8 for the psalmist's hymn of praise, repeated by the Church for the Resurrection of her Founder.

The melody starts with the eighth Psalm Tone intonation, working upward from the tonic G to the dominant *c* through a well-defined *torculus* on the tonic accent of *Jubiláte*, on to the *distropha* on the modal dominant, thus giving an effect of elation to the tonic accent of *ómnes*, so that *all* on earth might hear and rejoice. The spring of a fourth from the modal tonic to the dominant on the tonic accent of *psálmum*, followed by the prolonged dominant on the atonic syllable, is echoed for the first two syllables of the first *allelúia*. This prolongation on *c*, consisting of an extended *virga*, a *distropha* and the first note of a *clivis* (interpreted as a *pressus*) produces a strong tonal effect of jubilation, especially when rendered with the slight *tremulo* accorded the *strophicus* by singers of the " Golden Age " of plainchant. The melody remains symbolically on high for the concluding words of the Antiphon proper. The tonic accent of the climactic word *glóriam* is highly accentuated with the characteristic *quilisma a-b-c*.

The musical setting of the three final " allelúias " is a classic example of variety in melodic expression. The first *allelúia* works downward, the second upward, where the third one takes over on the note just released, and soars up to the dominant, which is repeated with a prolonged *virga*, before descending for the final cadence — magnificent graphic portrayal of a jubilant soul whose " Praise the Lord " becomes ever more inspiring as the song progresses.

The texts and chant of the Mass liturgy keep pace with the Church as she advances in joy with the Paschal Season. The melody of the Introit *Vócem jucunditátis* of the fifth Sunday after Easter (830) tries to outdo itself in describing " the voice of joy. " The text of this Introit is taken from Isaiah. As already stated, some of the earliest Introits have used texts from Holy Scripture that are not taken from the Psalms.

Even a glance at this Introit portrays its florid psalmodic intonation. From the opening tonic of the Mode, E, the melody moves swiftly upward through *jucunditátis* to the modal dominant, c, repeating this note up to the cadence notes of the word *annuntiáte*. From here a new melodic ascent arises in symbolic manner for the significant word *audiátur*, that the voice of joy man be *heard* by all.

The most effective melodic symbolism in the song occurs at the words *extrémum térrae*, where the motif, in keeping with the former word, rises to the extreme of the modal scale on the expressive composite neum which graces the tonic accent of the word *extrémum*. The modal dominant *punctum* on the tonic accent of *liberávit*, used as prepared note through its repetition of the final note of the preceding *quilisma*, receives thereby more emphasis than if it had been highly decorated. An artistic contrast is again effected through the varied melodic line of the two closing " allelúias, " the first motif in general descending direction, the second in ascending. The triple *quilisma* in repetition and sequence in the prolonged melisma of the final *allelúia* gives the impression of a " Praise Yaweh " started here below and continued in eternity. This inspiring melody is applied in large part to the Introit *Gáudens gaudébo* (1316) of the late Feast of the Immaculate Conception. For composition of this Mass Dom Pothier put words to already existing melodies.

The Church arrives at Christ's final appearance on earth with the Ascension Introit *Víri Galilaéi* (846), a further portrayal of impressive drama in words and melody. For the song of Our Lord's Ascension the highest of the Modes has appropriately been chosen, 7. From the initial note of the modal tonic G, the melody ascends. It remains in a high range through *admirámini*, as the astonished disciples gazing upwards at the heavens where the Master has just disappeared, stand motionless in marvel at the miracle which has just taken place before their eyes. The modal dominant *d* is used singly on the three preceding syllables of the tonic accent of *admirámini*, as preparation for its entrance on the first note of the composite neum at this place. This ornamentation on the tonic accent is immediately proportioned with a neum of like dimension on the following syllable of the same word. It would be contrary to the principles of liturgical plainchant to isolate an accented syllable by according it even a short composite neum, while setting all the preceding and following syllables of the same word in syllabic chant. In every aspect of this work the element of proportion prevails.

The melody makes an abrupt descent of a fifth from the tonic accent of *aspiciéntes*, in order that it may ascend symbolically for *caélum*. It remains in a high range, but in this course, through a slight preceding melodic descent, the song writer manages to give a melodic ascent also to *ascendéntem*, remaining in the upper register for the repeated *caélum*, following which the melody descends symbolically for *véniet* — the second coming of Christ.

The closing " allelúias " offer further example of this thrice-uttered acclamation clothed in striking melodic variety. The first *allelúia* soars but a degree below the summit of the Mode; the second drops contrastingly to a degree below the modal tonic, while the third makes an artistic compromise, modulating between the high and the low.

In order to analyze the pieces of the Mass Proper in their respective antiphonal and responsorial categories, we shall continue with the former group before approaching the latter. In the celebration of the Mass these two types of song are intermingled.

History

According to the testimony of St. Augustine (d. 430) the Offertory was born at the same time when antiphonal singing reigned everywhere, a fact which supports the supposition that it came into existence about the same time as the Introit, and at its origin was an antiphonal chant.

The absence of the Offertory chant from the Mass of Holy Saturday shows that the Roman liturgy did not possess it from the beginning. But all the Latin liturgies from the beginning have a chant at this place in the Mass, to fill up the time when the people offered their gifts. Even the officiating Pope had to bring his gift; the singers brought only the water that was mixed with wine (*Ordo Romano*, I). The ceremony of the offering of the people was at first universal. It soon disappeared from the Oriental liturgies but was retained in the Latin ones for a long time. [1]

The obligation to take part in the Offertory procession was still urged in ecclesiastical synods as late as the eleventh century, after which these admonitions of the bishops are no longer heard. Recent studies, which, however, are not complete, seem to prove that this disappearance of the Offertory procession may be dated at sometime about the year 1200. Today it is only the rite for the consecration of a bishop and in the analogous blessings of an abbott that we retain a solemn Offertory procession in a reduced form. [2]

Form

Dom A. Dohmes of Maria Laach suggests that since it may have been difficult for the people to sing and carry their gifts to the altar at the same time, this may account for the fact that the Offertory was the first of the antiphonal chants of the Mass to be taken over entirely by the *schola*, a change which occurred

---

[1] P. WAGNER, *op. cit.*, p. 107.

[2] Theodor KLAUSER, *A Brief History of the Liturgy* (Collegeville, Minn. : The Liturgical Press, 1953).

before Gregory I. It was from then on transformed into a responsorial piece for soloist and choir. Wagner states that since the choir members themselves had to carry their offerings to the altar, the execution of the verse was confided to but one or two singers, cantors, and the choir sang only the refrain. This produced a very interesting cyclical structure. It started with the Antiphon, or Refrain, sung by the *schola*, followed by one, two, or at most four Psalm verses sung by the cantors. The number of verses was fixed by the length of the offering. After each verse the *schola* repeated the last part of the Antiphon. At the end the entire Antiphon was sung by all : A-B*a*-C*a*-D*a*-A. [1]

There is a peculiarity of this chant which Wagner brings out, namely, that it is the only one of the liturgical pieces of the Mass and the Office which occasionaly repeats suitable words, or combinations of words, without being directed to do so by the liturgical text of the chant. Wagner makes the commentary that in all other cases the melody is wedded to the words of the text ordered by the Church, without altering their arrangement or repeating any part, and thus the liturgical chant grew up and developed in the closest connection with the liturgical text. The repetition of a word, where the liturgy does not order it, implies a certain revolt from it; it denotes the triumph of a subjective conception of the liturgical words. " But, " he continues, " it is not necessary to judge the repetition in the Offertories so severely. They were, it may be said, of a more speculative nature and were demanded by the length of the ceremonies of the offering. The value the repetition of a word or thought may have, viewed from an artistic standpoint, was shown later by compositions of the harmonized vocal music, for they made of it one of their most forcible methods of expression. However, artistic considerations are not the cause of the repetitions of the old Offertories. " [2]

These repetitions go back to a distant age; they exist in the Ambrosian Chant also. Some were sung throughout the Middle

---

[1] P. WAGNER, *op. cit.*, p. 111.

[2] *Ibid.*, p. 109.

Ages and are still to be found in the pre-Tridentine printed Graduals. The Tridentine Commission for the reform of the Missal struck out most of them. Only two remain, in both of which the first part of the text is repeated at the end : the Offertory *Dómine in auxílium* (1046) and *De profúndis* (1076). In addition, the Roman liturgy contains the following four Offertories wherein the repetition is immediate : *Jubiláte Déo ómnis térra* (480), *Jubiláte Déo univérsa térra* (486), *Benedíctus es... túas* (514), *Precátus est Móyses... díxit* (1030). [1]

The original Offertory melodies were simple, like those of the first Introits and Communions, but in the transmitted manuscripts they are melismatic, florid in character, more on the order of the Tract, Gradual and Alleluia. The structure of the verses is considered by Carl Ott as superior to the verses of the Gradual. " Certainly they represent a dramatic climax in the development of the chant, which stands in marked contrast to the quiet greatness of the earlier melodies, a contrast not dissimilar to that of Beethoven and Bach.... The Offertory verses can safely be assigned to the second half of the ninth century, perhaps, in their final form, even to the tenth century. They give the impression of having been created at a definite place (Metz?) at the instigation of a monk whose musical daring may well be compared to that of Beethoven. " [2]

When the ceremony of the congregational offering ceased (c. 1200), the Psalm verses were eliminated and the Antiphon, or Refrain, stood alone. From the thirteenth and fourteenth centuries the Offertory everywhere was but a single piece. The Requiem Mass (a later one) with its Offertory verse is the only reminder of the ancient usage. From the reaction exercised on music by liturgical things, it thus resulted that the Offertory became a very developed song of the soloist, as is found in the Gregorian Offertory. Accordingly, this piece became the artistic central point of the Mass, in taking over the function formerly filled by the *Gradual responsorium*.

---

[1] P. WAGNER, *op. cit.*, p. 111.

[2] W. APEL, *op. cit.*, pp. 375, 513.

Practically any one of the Offertories may be used as a specimen of psalmodic form among the pieces of the Proper of the Mass. For example, the intonation of the Offertory *Glória et honóre* (1137) starts on the mediant of Mode 1, F, as does Psalm Tone I. It then works up in florid psalmodic manner to the dominant *a* and proceeds toward its first full-stop cadence. Two temporary cadences, including the one of the intonation, precede the mediant full-stop cadence at *éum.* From here the melody takes up again on the dominant *a,* as does Psalm Tone I after its mediant cadence. Four phrases follow, the last of which closes on the modal tonic D, final note for three of Psalm Tone I endings.

The characteristic intonation described in the section on Antiphon form, D-*a*-*b♭*-*a*, is used for a great number of Offertory intonations, such as *Confitébor tíbi... Déus, Jubiláte Déo univérsa, Confitébur... in tóto córde, Benedícam Dóminum, In conspéctu, Benedícite Dóminum* (448, 486, 573, 1004, 1546, 1664), etc. These intonations are all preceded by two preparatory notes.

In the Offertory *Magníficat* (1670) the intonation motif is repeated at the start of the second phrase (after *et*), giving it the flavor of a Solemn Canticle Tone, wherein every verse starts with the intonation.

In the Sundays after Pentecost the Offertories follow numerically the order of the Psalms up through the seventeenth Sunday.

Tonality

All eight Modes are used in the Offertories. The beautiful Offertory *Recordáre Vírgo* (1637) is an example of pure Mode I, without *b♭*. The mixture of Modes also obtains, just as we have seen for the Introits. For examples, in the Offertory *Térra trémuit* (781), attributed to Mode 4, Mode 1 is predominant in the cadences. In fact, Mode 4 is not definitely established until the close of the cadence at the last two syllables of *allelúia.* A Mode in its Authentic and Plagal setting, or vice versa, is less a feature of the Offertory pieces.

The process of adaptation is used in the Offertories, but centonization is not one of its factors. The Offertories are pieces of a quite individual stamp.

The melody of the Offertory 1) *Constítues éos* (1520) is adapted to the text of the Offertory of the Feast of the Holy Trinity, 2) *Benedíctus sit* (911), the Introit of which Mass has already been analyzed in its adapted setting. The melody of the initial word in each piece is identical, but the rhythm of the two words is diverse, that which makes it impossible to obtain a like identical rhythmic adaptation for both settings. In the original version, 1, the tonic accent of *Constítues* is prominently asserted with a prolonged *punctum* (because it is isolated) followed by a *torculus* at the degree of a third, while the tonic accent of *Benedíctus* of 2 is supported by a *torculus* at the summit of the motif, thereby giving it due importance. The motif of the significant word *príncipes* of 1 is adapted to the likewise significant word *Páter* of 2. In view of the lesser syllable in the latter, the first two neums of *príncipes* are united for the tonic accent of *Páter* into a composite neum incorporating a *pressus*.

The vital composite neum on the tonic accent of *ómnem* in 1, with its spring of a fourth up to the summit of the melody, is symbolic portrayal of the height and breadth of the *whole* earth over which the Apostles are made princes. The same neum would undoubtedly have been adapted to the tonic accent of *unigénitus* in 2, had addition of the enclitic *que* to this word not shifted its tonic accent to the penult syllable. As it is, the secondary accent at this place receives the aforenamed neum, and the tonic accent is adapted to the rolling *torculus resupinus* of the tonic accent of *térram* in 1.

Each song of the following phrase of both 1 and 2 have the same number of syllables and an identical melodic motif; but, whereas the first word of the phrase in 1 is a dactyl and the second a spondee, it is exactly the reverse in 2. Notwithstanding, despite the diversity of verbal accentuation in the motif in question, not only are the tonic accents of both texts excellently

81

ornamented, but the remaining syllables of the same phrase are in absolute melodic proportion.

The following phrase to the full-stop in 1, at *nóminis túi*, contains five syllables, as compared to four syllables for 2 at this place, for *Sánctus quóque*. The adapted version has retained the same notes used for *nóminis* of 1, but for the final syllable of *Sánctus* of 2, the third note of the *tristropha* and the first note of the *podatus* on the last two syllables of *nóminis* are united into a *podatus* in 2 followed by the final note of the *podatus* of *nóminis* used as an isolated *virga*. This manipulation brings the word *quóque* in 2 in perfect line with *túi* in 1.

In the following phrase, the motif of *in ómni* in 1 is mirrored for *Spíritus* of 2, except for substitution of a final *clivis* in 2 for a *punctum* in 1. This permits a better cadence for 2, whereas the text does not call it in 1. However, the accentual setting at this place in 1 is superior to that of 2. The motif of *progénie* in 1, including two consecutive ascending fourths, is adapted to *quia fécit* in 2, again with substitution of a final *clivis* in 2, a degree lower than the one for *quóque*.

From here on to the close of each piece the number of syllables in 1 is seven, compared to eleven in 2. The adapter takes care of this diversity through melodic repetition, with slight mutation, of the motif of *Spíritus* for *nobíscum*, both of 2. This repetition does not occur in 1. After the appoggiatura on *et* in 1, the two texts of the melodies meet on the first syllable of *generatióne* of 1 and the like syllable of *misericórdiam* of 2. To the close of the songs there are still two more syllables in 2 than in 1. This condition is managed by according an extra note to 2 on the final syllable of *misericórdiam*, and in adapting the motif on the last syllable of *generatióne* of 1 to the first syllable of *súam* in 2. There is still slight mutation of the original melody at this place in 2, but the two versions meet at the *clivis* in varied quadruple setting at the final cadence of both songs.

The intricacies involved in an adaptation such as the above would seem to merit our esteem, unless it might be shown wherein something better could be effected with the same melody and diverse texts.

Compare also *Confírma hoc* (882) with the adapted version, *Sacerdótes Dómini* (949) of Corpus Christi. It is also interesting to study the like text (except for one word) of the Offertory and Communion *Scápulis súis* (537) in their respective songs. Although tonally related through their mutual dominant and melodic similarities, as already pointed out for Modes 3 and 8, nevertheless, in the chants themselves the melodic and rhythmic treatment of each text is entirely individual.

Melodic Procedures for Expressive and Symbolic Elements

The Offertory *Jubiláte* (486) is a masterpiece of musical science and artistry. It is an entirely original composition, and is one of the Offertories outside Paschal Time with an " allelúia " at its close. " The Church is exultant at the consolation of the Deity. Salvation has come and the Church exults interiorily after the long darkness of expectant centuries " (Dom Joseph Gajard).

One *jubiláte* proclamation is not sufficient. There is an immediate repetition of the first line of the Psalm verse, a particularity already stated in the section on form. The song writer manifests this excess of joy in inspiring manner. The opening *jubiláte* starts the song in motion with an uplifting intonation, after which the second jubilates on the tonic accent of the repeated acclamation with a melisma so long it would seem to extend to the very portals of heaven itself. This has been acclaimed one of the most celebrated passages of classical Roman style in Gregorian Chant. It embodies a range from low C to high *f*.

A beautiful sequence is effected through the diverse melodic setting of the three words, *veníte, audíte, narrábo,* as they follow in textual order. Every tonic accent in this song has received particular melodic application : striking evidence of the vital role played by the rhythm of the word in formation of the earliest Church chants. It is not necessarily the number of notes that determines the importance of the tonic accent. The form of a neum or a strong modal or strengthened note also have part

83

in this, as the *porrectus* for the tonic accent of *timétis*, and the prepared note for the tonic accent of *Dóminus*.

The relatively florid character of the Offertory melody in general precludes its melodic characteristics from symbolizing to the same degree the elements of sadness or distress expressed in the Introit melodies. At the same time, the Offertory does not "herald" the sentiment of the feast as the Introit does. It results, therefore, that the texts of the Offertories and Communions are extracted from Psalm passages of a more hopeful nature, even during the seasons of penance, than are the texts of the Introit.

For the first Sunday of Lent, therefore, nothing other than a spirit of hope and trust prevails in all the pieces of the Proper, the Tract included. The Offertory *Scápulis* (537) of this Sunday offers examples of uplifting melody for expressive words such as *obumbrábit tibi* and *pénnis éjus*. The tonic accent of the final word of protective assurance, *scúto*, is a sequence to the composite neum of *pénnis*, but a degree higher as the psalmist's song augments in trust in the Lord.

An enveloping type of neum rolls symbolically around the syllables of the word *circumdábit*, leading into the key-word *véritas*. Its highly ornamented tonic accent lends emphasis to the term that portrays the intrinsic nature of God—His Essence.

The Offertory of the second Sunday of Lent, *Meditábor* (548), presents interesting melodic play. The motif of *mandátis* is repeated, with slight mutation, for *mandáta*, a reflection of leitmotiv. The four opening notes of this motif are used also for *levábo*, for whose tonic accent the strong *pressus* gives the word an element of uplift, as the psalmist "lifts up his hands to the commandments which he has loved." Note the long and persistent melisma on the tonic accent of the climactic word *diléxi*, the key which unlocks the divinely revealed law.

It is not the importance of a word taken by itself that determines its significance in a text, but it is the modifying influence that this word expresses in the entire subject matter that gives it its particular value. Thus in the Offertory

84

Impropérium (600) the most pronounced motif is accorded the repeated *non*, an anguished cry symbolically portrayed in rhythmically urgent neums at the summit of the song.

As the Church enters the joy of the Easter Season the melodies of her chant unfold with the spirit of the liturgy, as we have seen for the Introit. The jubilatory character of the Offertory *Angelus Dómini* (787) incorporates striking examples of melodic symbolism.

The intonation works up to the seventh degree of the modal scale, *c*, and then descends only for the melody to rise again at *Dómini* with its well-ornamented tonic accent. The final note of this word, *a*, is repeated as an appoggiatura for the *pressus* on the tonic accent of *descéndit*, which sets in motion a melisma that runs down a degree below the gamut of the modal scale, thus picturing the Angel of the Lord who " came down from heaven. " A new melisma takes up from the low C where the former left off, then works up to prepare for the tonic accent of *caélo*, where the melody soars symbolically heavenward until it reaches high *e*, at which place it enters and remains in Mode 7 through *muliéribus*, where it takes its repeated flight on the tonic accent of the word that portrays the heroines of this glorious drama.

On the tonic accent of the word *illúxit* in the Offertory *Benedíctus qui vénit* (806) the melody takes a dramatic *salicus* spring into the region of light of the Authentic Mode.

A further example of melodic symbolism which reaches toward the heights is the intonation of the Offertory for the Feast of the Ascension, *Ascéndit Déus* (849). Up through the first note of the *clivis* on *Déus*, melodic and rhythmic beauty is made possible through nothing other than an ascending eight-note diatonic scale, by reason of both the tonality expressed in the arsic portion of the neums, and the variety of rhythmic combination among them. I know of no manner in which melodic science and art could be so satisfyingly expressed with such limited matter, other than by means of free-ryhthm modal plainchant.

85

Thus, following the intonation, the melody continues to mount. The tonic accent of *Déus* is decorated with a short melisma starting with the characteristic *quilisma a-b-c*, followed by a second one a degree lower. This melodic lift prepares the sentiment of rejoicing expressed in the climactic word *jubilatióne* with its series of jubilatory neums on the tonic accent, each capped with high *c*, a procedure that lends a flavor of persistence to the word of rejoicing that would draw the whole world with it.

In the cadence of the Offertory *Pópulum húmilem* (1015), ingenuity is displayed in the closing melisma, through the triple appearance of the same motif, diversified through slight melodic variance of the *climacus* of the first two settings, and the *torculus* and *clivis* of the third setting.

Beautiful melodic symbolism is portrayed in the Offertory *Super flúmina* (1065), through the descending flowing melisma on the word *flúmina*. The melisma on the word *Babylónis* takes up in classic contrary movement where the previous one leaves off.

Melodic symbolism is likewise evident in the Offertory *De profúndis* (1076), where the intonation emerges from the depths of the first note of the lowest modal gamut, A. The repetition in the text of this Offertory was pointed out in the section on form.

A beautiful melisma that might well serve for a vocal exercise graces the tonic accent of the word *Vírgo* in the Offertory *Beáta es Vírgo* (1272), and likewise the tonic accent of the key-word *Dóminus* in the Offertory *Ave María* (1268). In the latter piece this key-word with that of *María* receive the most inspiring melismata in the song.

The Church certainly has a special predilection for her martyrs. In codification of the liturgy they follow the Apostles and Evangelists. She keeps ever before the eyes of her faithful that without the shedding of blood she would have neither a Founder nor consequent establishment through His followers. So she rejoices and mourns not over her heroes who victoriously entered the portals of eternal life to receive their everlasting crowns of glory. Witness the exceptional "allelúias" at the close of the Offertories of Masses I and III of the Common of Martyrs outside Paschal Time (1165, 1172).

The intonation of the majestic Offertory *Mirábilis Déus* of Mass I (1165) goes straight up to *Déus* and remains in the upper range for the entire song. The tonic accents of the powerful words *virtútem* and *fortitúdinem* are ably supported with strong melismatic neums which transcend the upper range of the Mode. This lofty hymn of praise to God, wonderful in His saints, closes with its joyful *allelúia* on a long flowing melisma. In rendition the antepenult syllable of this word, as unaccented syllable, should be deposited with its proportionate dynamic quality at the *arsis* of the first *torculus*, after which rhythmic unit the pure vocal part of the melisma can have its own way from the standpoint of dynamism, in according more impulse to the melodically higher *arsis* of the *clivis* than is given to the first note of the *porrectus* on the tonic accent of the word. In other words, the syllables of the word must first be respected in their relative rhythmic dynamism of the word as a whole, before the melody can take wings and assert its particular melodic and rhythmic importance. Let us ever bear in mind that Gregorian Chant is the *prayer* sung, not the *song* prayed (St. Pius X).

We find melodic symbolism likewise expressed in the Offertory *Confitebúntur* (1148), where on the word *caéli* the melody mounts steadily to the summit of the highest Mode.

Justórum ánimae (1172), from Mass III of the Common of Martyrs, is an Offertory with the potentialities of a magnificent overture. The intonation works upward, subsequently highlighting the word *ánimae*. The word *Déi* proves its counterpart. A broken seventh is used in the motif for the conjunction *et,* where the melody rises from the tonic D to the seventh *c* through the intervals of a minor, a major and a minor third. This would seem to prepare the singer emotionally for the sinister words *torméntum malítiae,* expressed symbolically in the lowest register of the Mode, as is the continuing text expressing the blindness of the unwise.

87

As the climax arrives and transformation of the torments of evil are revealed, the singer is again prepared emotionally, but now for a contrary reason, with a repeated broken seventh, this time by way of a major fifth and a minor third. From here the melody takes off in a developed melisma with repeated high *c*s at arsic points, like a jubilant soul who is impelled to repeat the same thing over and over until it is sure that all are listening to hear the glad tidings. This accomplished, the melody calms down to reveal where God's victims are found eternally—they are " in peace. " The *allelúia* which follows is expressed in a subdued melodic pattern in keeping with the tranquil sentiment of the closing text.

In the Offertory *Tu es Pétrus* (1333) the aforesaid broken seventh, all in thirds, is used in the motif for the significant word *aedificábo*. A further feature of this song is its use of the text of the first half of the Tract of the same Mass. Here is seen added example of the melodic and modal variety expressed in two like texts of dissimilar chants, each setting scientifically and artistically respected for the rhythmic and melodic integrity of the whole.

The Offertory *Quis ascéndet* (1495), among untold others, offers interesting symbolic procedures for expressing the sentiment of the liturgical text. The initial notes of the intonation, G-*c*, spring up a fourth to the modal dominant, setting the stage for the ascent. The *quilisma* which supports the tonic accent of the word *ascéndet* starts a third below the note just left, in order to rise back symbolically to it. The tonic accent of *móntem* climbs up to *e*, summit of the Mode and highest point in the melody, reflection of " the mountain of the Lord. " At *lóco* two composite neums, the latter tending upward, prepare a beautiful melisma of varied movement, setting on high the tonic accent of *sáncto*, " His holy place, " where the Lord awaits " the innocent of hands and the pure of heart. "

In the Offertory *Stétit Angelus* (1656) a magnificent symbolic melisma, starting off with a broken seventh, composed of a major fifth and a minor third, sets on high the tonic accent of the word *ascéndit*. Note also in the Offertory *Cum ésset* (1685)

88

the uplifting melismata reserved for the key-words *Maria* and *Joseph*. The Mass from which this Offertory is taken was not instituted until 1931.

It might be added by way of conclusion to this series of Offertories, that very worthy chant labor, mostly in adaptation, has been effected by liturgical musicians of our times, men imbued with the science, art and tradition of the uniquely unsurpassable melodies which took birth and developed with the life of the Church itself. This later work is produced for the new Masses which enter the liturgical calendar through decrees of the Holy See.

Let us picture to ourselves the inspiring beauty of execution these classic chants must have received during the " Golden Age " of rendition by chanters exercised from boyhood into the mysteries of this sacred music. These men knew no other type of song, hence their well-disciplined voices as well as their entire spiritual formation produced an artistry that we in our labyrinth of music of succeeding generations know only through tradition.

COMMUNION

History

The first information we have regarding the Communion comes to us from St. Cyril of Jerusalem (347-8), which indicates that the first half of verse 9 of Psalm 33, " O taste and see that the Lord is sweet, " was used at that time as the text of the Communion. The Apostolic Constitutions (4th c.) give all of Psalm 33 for the Communion : " Psalm 33 should be sung while all the others communicate. " St. John Chrysostom relates from his journeys in Antioch (387-397) that those initiated in the mysteries (the faithful) repeat assiduously, " ' The eyes of all hope in Thee, O Lord, and Thou givest them meat in due season ' (Ps. 144, 15), sung as a refrain. This takes place while they savor the Body and Blood of Him Who regenerated the faithful. " St. Jerome speaks of the song in Bethlehem (408-10), which was evidently a collective one : " Associated each day

with the Celestial Bread we sing 'Taste and see....'"
St. Augustine in his sermons always returns to, "Approach
the Lord and you will be enlightened," as well as to verse 9
of Psalm 33.

Form

In Africa the Communion Psalm was sung like the Offertory,
by the people. At Rome antiphonal singing of the Communion
by the people must have prevailed at the same time as that of
the Introit, since the Antiphons of each seem to be from the
same period. Each had its origin in antiphonal singing of
a Psalm, one at the beginning of the Mass, the other at the end.
Furthermore, the Communion verses were always sung to the
Tones of the Introit. Thus the structure of each must have
been the same. The number of Communion Psalm verses was
decided by the time occupied with the distribution of the Holy
Eucharist.

At Rome the chant of the Communion was evidently assigned
to the *schola* at an early age, because the first Roman ordo speaks
of its rendition by the subdeacon and *schola*, to whom it had
already passed a long time before. Also at this early period
Psalms other than 33 were chosen for its rendition. The Roman
Mass uses verse 9 only for the Communion of the eighth Sunday
after Pentecost.

Fom the eleventh century the giving out of Holy Communion at High Mass gradually went out of practice, so there
was eventually no necessity for a long accompaniment, and
from that time the manuscripts begin to leave out the verses.
Those of the twelfth century seldom have them.

As with the other chants so with the Communion, the
original form was conserved longest in Germany, where
thirteenth century manuscripts of the Thomas Kirche in Leipzig
give the verses for all the days of the Church year. From the
fourteenth century they disappeared and the Antiphon stood
alone as the Communion piece. [1] The Requiem Mass with

---

[1] P. WAGNER, *op. cit.*, p. 119.

its single verse reminds us of the ancient usage. As in het case of the Offertories, the Communions of the Sundays after Pentecost conserve the mounting numerical order of the Psalms, 9, 12, 16, 17, etc., with, however, inclusion of a few non-psalmodic texts.

The psalmodic form is present in the Communion, as in the remaining pieces of the Mass Proper. For example, the Communion *Pánem caéli* (1495) is clear portrayal of this formula. The intonation is that of Psalm Tone 8, leading up to the modal dominant *c*, which obtains in psalmodic fashion to the mediant cadence at the full-stop, after *éis*. The tonic leads up to the dominant in the two subsequent phrases, the latter of which closes on the modal tonic G.

An example of the quatenary type of melody, described in the section on form for the Antiphon, is seen in the Communion *Amen díco vóbis* (1077): four melodic phrases with three intervening note modulations. The first phrase closes on *a*, dominant of Mode 1, the second on G, subdominant, the third on F, mediant, and the final phrase on D, tonic of the Mode.

The Communion Antiphon is less developed than the Introit Antiphon, which, as already stated, announces the character of the feast which the Mass celebrates. The average Communion resembles more the melodic type of the Office Antiphon. However, the ornate type is not entirely absent, as seen in a Communion such as *Pánem de caélo* (1035), and *Quam mágna* (1480).

For a long time the Communion has been sung after the communion of the priest; at least that is the rule. Wagner gives as reason for this that perhaps it came about through the fact that the Antiphon only very seldom contains any longer any reference to the Holy Communion *(item)*.

Tonality

All eight Modes a e employed in the Communion song. However, Mode 1 predominates. At the same time great ambiguity reigns in definition of the Communion modalities. No other type of Mass chant includes such a large percentage of melodies showing tonal instability, about one-fifth of the whole.   In making these latter statements, Willi Apel supports them with the example of the Communion *De frúctu* (1031), assigned to Mode 6 in the current chant editions.   Aurelian of Roémé in his *Musica disciplina* (c. 850) and Regino, Abbot of Prüm (d. 915) in his *Tonarius* ascribe it to Mode 3, as does the Gradual of Corbie.   In the *Tonarius* of Berno of Reichnau (d. 1048) and in the Sarum Gradual it appears as Mode 8, and in Guido's *Tonarius* (of the 11th century) as Mode 1, while the Montpellier Codex (11th century) places it in Mode 6.   Apel comments that it is difficult to say what caused such an appalling disagreement other than it, no doubt, underwent certain changes in the ninth, tenth and later centuries.   This possibly resulted as well in its half-tone cadence on F, apparently an isolated case in the Mass Propers. [1]   However, Apel's statement must refer to a *final* cadence only, for we shall run into this cadence in the course of 4th Mode Communions.   A final half-tone cadence occurs in the 6th Mode Antiphon *Vírgo pótens* (1679), as example outside the Mass.

As examples of modal uncertainty, the following Communions might be cited : *Meménto vérbi túi* (1065) attributed to Mode 4, wherein Mode 2 is very pronounced from the beginning of the intonation up to the cadence neum on *dedísti*, at which place to the end Mode 4 appears.   Note the half-tone cadence to F at the close of the first phrase.   In one of the longest Communions, *Tanto témpore* (1450), ascribed to Mode 4, Modes 1 and 2 are strongly asserted during the course of the melody, despite the intermingling of Mode 4 cadences to E, of which there are but three among eleven melodic cadences, including a half tone cadence to F, at *est*.

The Communion *Pásser invénit* (556) is transposed up a fifth in the notation, in order to avoid an *e♭* on the *torculus* for the second syllable of *púllos*.

---

[1] W. APEL, *op. cit.*, pp. 168, 265.

Adaptation

A late but worthy adaptation is that of the Christmas Communion
1) *Vidérunt ómnes* (410) to the Communion text *Cor méum* (1474)
of the Feast of St. Philip Neri.

The diversity between the number of syllables in the
intonations is, 1) 5 versus 2) 3; hence the only expressed tonic
accent in 2, at *méum*, is adapted to the first tonic accent of 1,
at *Vidérunt*. In 2 the tonic accent on the monosyllabic substantive
Cor, in this setting, would not be rendered in discourse.

In the following phrase the number of syllables and the
verbal rhythm is the same in both texts, with exception of the
conjunction *et* in 2, which additional monosyllable receives
a double appoggiatura in the form of a *podatus*. In the same
phrase the two tonic accents of 1 are of equal importance, and
are so treated melodically. Although at this place in 2 the tonic
accent of *cáro* is of greater importance than that of *méa*, the
salicus on the tonic accent of the former word is of sufficient
dynamism to retain its due proportion.

But one word is contained in the following short phrase
of each song, *salutáre* in 1, *exsultavérunt* in 2. The first, and
extra, syllable in the latter is adapted to a double appoggiatura
in the form of a *podatus*. The four remaining syllables coincide
rhythmically and melodically with 1. The tonic accent of
these key-words in both songs receives a like composite neum
of tremendous vigor, a prolonged *virga* (because it is isolated)
followed by the upward spring of a major triad with a concluding
neum. Thus, in the original text the purpose of the Incarnation—Salvation—is set forth in the fullness of its significance.
(The word *salutáre* receives an identical melodic treatment
in the Christmas Vigil Communion, *Revelábitur*, 362.) A feeling
of exultation permeates the entire setting of 2 through the
power of the same melodic setting for *exsultavérunt*.

By means of a preparatory note on *in* of 2, because of its
additional syllable in this phrase, the words *Déum* and *Déi*
meet melodically in both chants as the same term but with
a variance of declension.

In view of the quality of even a " Silver Age " adaptation such as this, one is persuaded that the adapters of liturgical plainchant must have sought carefully throughout the texts and melodies of the already existing repertory before putting their finger on just the right melody for adaptation to a new text.

Centonization occurs in a certain number of Communion songs in the realm of the texts. The Communion for the Feast of St. Stephen, Martyr, *Vídeo caélos* (418), offers an example. It is made up of three different extracts from chapter seven of the Acts. The final phrase is taken from Luke, 23, an echo of the Savior's last cry on the Cross. The text of one of the shortest Communions, *Spíritus qui* (892), is taken from two parts of St. John with reinforcement of a third part. [1]

Melodic Procedures for Expressive and Dramatic Elements

When, in the Communion *Vídeo caélos* Stephen cries out to the Lord to accept his spirit, the melody cries out with him. There is a sudden upward spring of a fifth on the tonic accent of *Dómine* that carries the word up beyond the dominant of the Authentic Mode, 7. The melody then remains in the tension of the upper range until the victim's appeal that this sin be not laid to the charge of his enemies, at which place the melody descends in keeping with the sentiment of the prayer itself. For the word *peccátum* the melody goes down symbolically to the lowest range of the Mode, after which it makes a gradual ascent to the closing modal tonic for the Saint's apology for his enemies, again in the words of the Crucified, for the men who stoned him to death. These last words are a litugical appendix. They do not occur in Stephen's story in the Acts.

As the Church enters the Christmas cycle she hastens to fete her infant martyrs, the first after the birth of the Savior. It is their blood that softened the earth for excavation for the foundation of the spiritual temple Christ came to lay upon earth. The Communion *Vox in Ráma* (430) celebrates this

---

[1] Jn 15, 26; 16, 14; 17, 5.

most glorious but agonizing of feasts. The tonic accents of the words of ultimate distress, *plorátus* and *ululátus*, are manifestly melodically symbolized, the former with a persistent *pressus*, the latter with a repeated *podatus* at the interval of a semi-tone, like the wail of a tormented soul in agony. The same musical effect is given to the *torculus resupinus* on the tonic accent of *plórans* followed by a semi-tone *clivis* on the atonic syllable.

A strong *pressus* at a half-step progression on *nóluit*, as a cry of despair, stresses that Rachael will *not* be comforted. The *quia* is long drawn out on a descriptive melisma, since the reason for Rachael's refusal to be comforted hangs on it—*because* they are *not*—a tragedy without human solution.

On the renowned occasion of the visit of the Wisemen from the East to the Crib, the Church celebrates the first manifestation of the Godhead of the Redeemer. The Communion of this feast, *Vídimus* (462), offers an interesting motif of Oriental flavor. The first two syllables of the word *Oriénte* are accompanied by a *salicus* and *punctum* which together form a perfect tritone in scale progression : F-*b*. However, the spring of the voice on G, because of the *salicus*, breaks the tritone tonality.

In contrast to the ascending initial motif which we observed in the Offertory *Ascéndit Jésus*, at Christ's Ascension, in the Communion *Descéndit Jésus* (473), adapted in large part to the melody of *Vidérunt ómnes* (410), the initial motif moves symbolically downward as the Child Jesus descends with His parents into Nazareth. The adapter made a happy choice as model melody.

A delightful example of melodic play is used in the transposed Communion *Pásser invénit* (556) (a piece already studied in the section on tonality), where the four-fold *podatus* for *et túrtur nídum* sways back and forth like the tune of a little lullaby sung by the turtle-dove to her young. It is true, as Willi Apel points out (*id.*, 303), that the liquescent neums at this place (which give it such a " lilting " flavor) take care of the double consonants. At the same time, there is no reason why they could not have been varied in form, for example, a *climacus*, *torculus* and *podatus* in liquescent form. However, it is precisely the fourfold *podatus* at this place which so satisfyingly gives the impression of the peaceful rhythm of a song of rest.

A most harmonious melodic setting of word sequence occurs in the Communion *Pétite* (843), for *pétite*, *quaérite* and *pulsáte*. The motives for these triple words of Christ's mandate reflect the relative degree of intensity which they signify. *Pétite* and *quaérite* are expressed with simple motives and modestly ornamented tonic accents. In contrast, the tonic accent of *pulsáte*, when the soul storms the heavens, is dynamically portrayed with a developed motif embracing a double *quilisma*, which, with its following prolongation on the atonic syllable manifests the unrelenting importunity of a soul, who, like the man in the Gospel persists in knocking at the door of his neighbor in the middle of the night until the unwilling occupant finally rises and gives him what he seeks, not because he is a friend, but because of the importunity of the man without. The motif for *pulsánti* is a slight variation of the one for *pulsáte*, with reflection of a leitmotiv.

The Communion *Amen díco vóbis quidquid* (1077) employs a melodic procedure similar to the one just cited, in augmentation of intensity for a sequence of terms. The word *pétitis* is accompanied by a calm little motif, whose *torculus* on the tonic accent and following notes on the remaining syllables rise and descend but one degree from the subdominant of the Mode, G. The *torculus* on the tonic accent of *crédite* starts one degree higher, with the following notes on the remaining syllables descending a third, that which gives this word more prominence. Following this the tonic accent of the climactic word *accipiétis* soars up in augmentation on a double *podatus*, then descends in contrary movement. The gradual unfolding of the two words of prayer and faith acts as a prelude for *accipiétis*, the essential—receiving.

An impressive example of the dramatic possibilities of liturgical plainchant with a minimum of material is found in the intonation of the Communion *Páter si non pótest* (601) on the outcry " Páter. " The extended setting of this word through the *distropha* on the tonic accent followed by the half-step *pressus* on the atonic syllable, accord it the lingering appeal of the cry of Gethsemane.

In the Communion *Fáctus est repénte* (882) for the Feast of Pentecost, a striking intonation proclaims the descent of the Holy Ghost upon the assembly in the Cenacle. The unexpected rise of a fifth, with its immediate succession in contrary movement, inversion, gives the startling effect of a great event happening suddenly. There is a symbolic rise for *de caélo* from the preceding note to the repeated upward fifth. This uncommon procedure of three identical consecutive intervals of such breadth, reflects in itself the unusual in the text. From *caélo* the melodic line still ascends for *sónus*, where, at the peak of the melody its *sound* is heard by all.

The tonic accent of *repléti* is prolonged with a *salicus* until the *fullness* of the indwelling of the Holy Spirit is sensed, after which the song expresses itself with a diversity of flowing neums on the tonic accents of *loquéntes* and *magnália*, followed by a broad cadence on *Déi*, as the inspired recipients of the tongues of fire go forth " speaking the mighty works of God. " This Communion melody is applied to the Communion text *Quotiescúmque* (950) of Corpus Christi, a thirteenth century Mass.

In the Communion *Unus mílitum* (975) the tonic accents of the key-words, *sánguis* and *áqua*, are portrayed on opposite melodic levels, *sánguis* in the heights, *áqua* in the depths, with well-defined tonic accents for each word. The elevated setting of *sánguis* and the lowered one of *áqua* could express in a mystical sense the union of Jesus Christ and the faithful, represented by the mingling of wine and water in the holy Sacrifice of the Mass, an interpretation given to this rite by theologians.

An interesting theoretic melodic procedure is used in the Communion *Díco vóbis* (984). Starting at *super*, three consecutive verbal accents are accompanied with the *punctum a*, mediant of Mode 5, all in downward progression, twice in whole-tone intervals, and once with a major third. Rhythmic monotony in rendition of this passage is avoided through arsic distinction of the relative importance of the three accents, the first as only

97

rhythmic accent, receiving the least dynamic quality, the second as tonic accent, the most, the third as secondary accent, an intermediary quality.

A similar procedure to the one just cited occurs in the Communion *Tu mandásti* (1062). The word *justificatióne* is accompanied by the same *torculus* starting on *a*, for both its ternary and secondary accents. Through relative dynamic distinction between the *arsis* of each of these neums, with the principle dynamic quantity on the highest note of the composite neum on the tonic accent, rhythmical proportion of this, the key-word, is perfectly preserved.

In the Communion *Qui mandúcat* (1019) a very effective *crescendo* works up to the significant word *sánguinem*, where it remains at the summit of the Mode until the cadence at *mánet*. Melodically the song could end here, but the remaining text gives the entire song the aspect of an antecedent and consequent.

A striking short melodic motif, tonally prepared by the preceding composite neum, is applied to the word *clámor* in the Communion *Quinque prudéntes* (1228). With this motif it emerges into the high range of the song with the cry that announces the coming of the Bridegroom, at which the virgins who are prepared with oil in their lamps will go forth to meet Christ the Lord. Note the element of thrill in this *exíte*, its tonic accent mounting to the summit of the Mode on a vigorous *quilisma*-neum.

At the close of a calm melodic run in normal intervals in the Communion *Jóseph fíli Dávid* (1404), the climactic word *Maríam* is set on high with the upward spring of a fourth, followed by a suave undulating *torculus* in the same range for the tonic accent. No other adornment is needed to highlight this name. The simplicity of its setting reflects the perfection of this attribute bestowed upon the betrothed of the foster father of Christ.

Melodic symbolism is interestingly depicted in the Communion *Tanto témpore* (1450). The low range melody through *Philíppe* portrays the disappointment in the Master's voice at Philip's failure to know Him as God after such a long association. Even the melodic cadence of the first question descends. The word *Pátrem* remains also in the low range. But when the doctrinal matter comes into focus, sadness gives way to firmness as Christ reveals the relation between the Father and the Son. The tonic accent of *égo* rises dramatically on a *salicus*. This time *Pátre* is set in an upper range with a short melisma for its cadence syllable, after which, following the tonic accent of *Páter*, the melody starts the descent down to the *me* of the God-man. At the second question *est* rises in normal fashion, on one of the leading-tone cadences in chant, E-F, allusion to which has already been made. The closing " allelúias " carry the melody to its tonic note of rest.

The text of the *Allelúia* of the same Mass is the same as that of the Communion, through *Pátrum*. However, both modal and rhythmic differentiations obtain between the two settings, giving each its individual character in keeping with the type of song in each case.

In the Communion *Per sígnum Crúcis* (1457) a soaring melody, rising to *g*, summit of the highest Mode, frees itself from its surrounding motives at the climax of the text with the words *líbera nos*, deliverance from the enemy at the sign of the Cross.

A less usual procedure is that of the intonation of the Communion *Quam mágna* (1480), which we have already seen in the section on form. A *torculus resupinus* starting on the modal dominant accompanies the initial word, melodic prelude for " greatness " as herald of the text. A very striking contrast in the same song is the prolonged rising melisma on the tonic accent of *abscondísti*, as opposed to a similarly developed melisma on the tonic accent of *timéntibus*, but in descending order, the latter depicting symbolically the lowliness of holy fear.

At times the melodic character on but one word of the song symbolizes the basic sentiment of the entire liturgical text. In the Communion *Tu púer* (1502) a unique motif is fashioned for the word *paráre*, one made up of a continuation of the modal tonic D applied singly on the preparatory syllable, as first note

99

of a repeated *pressus* form, and finally as first note of a *clivis* on the ultimate syllable. This individual setting in the midst of otherwise undulating motives draws immediate attention to the key-word of John's mission — one who *prepares* the way of the Lord.

The melody of the Communion *Sínite párvulos* (1616) enters calmly into movement, but with well-supported tonic accents, moving smoothly upward : lovely portrayal of the quiet with which Jesus spoke in order not to frighten the little children. Then, as His command becomes more vigorous the melody rises to its upper range. And when, as previously illustrated, His words take on a doctrinal character, here at *tálium*, the melodic contour suddenly changes. An unexpected rise of a fifth on the tonic accent of this word leads up on *est* into the range of the Authentic Mode 7. The developed ornamentation of the tonic accent of *régnum* followed by the broad *torculus* for the tonic accent of *Déi*, the two complimentary words of *tálium est*, leave no doubt that in these utterances are embodied the substance of that which the creature must become before he enters his Father's house : a little child — for of such is the kingdom of God.

The liturgy offers a most appropriate text for the humble and despised Joseph of Cupertina, a creature rejected not only by his own but even by the religious orders, but whom God raised to a pinnacle of such superior wisdom that he became the counselor of the great men of Italy, and died in a radiance of glory in 1664.

The psalmist has provided just the right text for this saint in the Communion *Ego sum páuper* (1647), and its melody is in perfect conformity with the sentiment of the Psalm. The brief ascent of a third at the intonation leads into a *porrectus* in the same modest orbit on the tonic accent of *páuper*. Then follows a symbolic descent for *dólens*. The double *clivis* of minor thirds on the tonic accent of this word actually *sings* affliction. Then as the psalmist turns his eyes upward at *sálus* toward the source of his help, the melody works up into a hymn of praise which transcends the Mode and rises to the Authentic 7 at *Laudábo*, where it remains aloft through *magnificábo*, then descends to Mode 8 for the cadence of the song. Herein is vivid textual and melodic portrayal of : " But your sorrow shall be turned into joy. "

When toward the end of the Pentecost Season the Church arrives at the great Feast of All Saints, the liturgy presents one of the most sublime texts of the New Testament for the Communion of this celebration, *Beáti múndo córde* (1727), from the Sermon on the Mount. The first *Beáti*, at the intonation, starts on *a*, modal dominant, and remains in the upper range of " the pure of heart " for the entire phrase. The motif for *beáti pacífici* moves peacefully in a lower range, beautifully ornamented, remaining however within the tranquil scope of a fifth. But when the text arrives at the harassing fate of God's victims in this valley of evil, the *beáti* takes a sudden energetic spring upward on a major triad leading into a *scandicus* on the tonic accent, soaring a degree beyond the upper tonic of the Mode : virile melodic portrayal of the terrible inner struggle undergone by the victims who with fortitude support the persecution of the wicked.

The repeated high *c* for the ternary and secondary accents of *persecutiónem*, followed by a third and fourth interval descent respectively, then leading up but one degree to the tonic accent, all in syllabic chant in an otherwise neumatic setting, reflect well the *unadorned persistence* of evil. There is, of course, no monotony in this setting if each verbal accent is given its relative dynamic quantity. This key-word stands out boldly in its present melodic vesture, as it should, for without persecution there would be little amends in this world for justice sake that would assure in its wake the Kingdom of Heaven.

I believe we can all agree that these short antiphonal chants offer examples of dramatic and symbolic play that is unexcelled in any musical literature that would attempt to compete with it within the scope of from six to eight diatonic notes.

History

St. Justin in his first Apology (c. 155) gives us the following description of the early Eucharistic Sacrifice: " On the day of the Sun all who dwell in the cities or in the country come together in one place. The narratives of the Apostles or the writings of the Prophets are read as long as time will permit. When the reader finishes, the president (the bishop) or his representative verbally instructs and exhorts all to follow the beautiful example just cited. Then all rise and prayers are said; finally, at the termination of the prayers, bread and water are brought. The president in like manner offers prayers and thanksgiving, according to his ability, and the people respond with the acclamation ' Amen. ' Each person receives a part of the Blessed Bread which is distributed and is sent to the absent by the ministers of the deacon. "

This account reveals, then, that the primitive Eucharistic Sacrifice started with readings of Holy Scripture, as in the Synagogue ritual of the Sabbath, and as still exists in the Roman Mass of the Presanctified. During the fifth century the Lessons at Rome were reduced to two, Epistle and Gospel, but the Psalms still remained two, although both were now joined together between the Epistle and Gospel. The first of the two Psalms produced the Gradual, and from the second the melismatic Alleluia verses resulted. The Gradual is the oldest Mass song. Together with the Tract, the earliest chants of the Mass are, then, the Lesson chants and the Gradual.

The name *Responsorium* was still used in the first Roman ordo for this early responsorial chant of the Mass, but some time in the Middle Ages the name " Gradual " came into existence from the fact that the reader who chanted the Psalm stood on a higher place, the step *(gradus)* of the ambo from which the subdeacon had read the Epistle, the privilege of going up into the ambo being reserved for the deacon, who read the Gospel. The idea of a higher place, raised on steps, remained. Later we shall see how the term " Gradual " became established.

The Apostolic Constitutions indicate three groups of readings in the early Church : 1) From the Old Testament; 2) The Acts or the Epistles of St. Paul; 3) The four Gospels. The same document states that the readings were interspersed with chants of the Psalms. After each couplet of readings from the Old Testament (in these groups of readings it seems they had many couplets) the people sang as far as the acrostic, the pause marked at the middle or end of the verse.

At this epoch one entire Psalm was sung, and this practice continued until the fifth century. St. Jerome and St. Augustine both allude to this custom. The Psalms were an echo of that which was taught by the readings, and the Fathers attached the greatest importance to the fact that the people understand what they sang.

Although the Gradual and Alleluia are not separated in the Missal, they are actually two independent compositions, as presented in the *Liber Gradualis*, and were, in their original rendition, separated by a reading, so that (following the Jewish custom) every reading was succeeded by a song. There is in general a difference of modal tonality between the Gradual and its immediately following song, as well. There are still days in the Roman liturgy when the original separation is retained. From the liturgical standpoint these responsorial Psalms completed the readings, so that a *solo* type of melody did not appear in the liturgy except when prepared by a reading.

The word *Psalmus* indicates the contents of the chant, which was a Psalm, while the Roman name *Responsorium* points out the method of performance. In its original rendition the Gradual was purely responsorial in form; the Respond, or Refrain, followed by its immediate repetition, then the Psalm verses, after which the Respond was sung again, for the third time : A-A-B-C-D-....A.

Eventually participation of the people in the chant of the Psalms after the readings disappeared. From the second half of the fifth century the *schola* of educated voices in the Church took over the singing of the Respond, and it in turn became quite as elaborate as the soloist's verses. The rendition now proved so beautiful and of such inspirational value that the bishop and his assistants did not proceed with the liturgical ceremonies but listened to the singing. The Gradual is thus an integral part of the Divine Service.

By the middle of the sixth century the music of the *Responsorium* was so elaborate that only one Psalm verse was sung after the introductory passage (Respond) was repeated. At the close of the Psalm verse the Respond was sung once again.

The abbreviation of the text stems from the period of the introduction of the full melismatic style in the Mass Respond, which came about between 450 and 550, as just stated. " In the Latin liturgy of the second half of the fifth century the melismatic style and the solo chant always appear together, just as antiphonal psalmody wears the simple form of melodic dress. " [1]

The immediate repetition of the Respond was not rigorously maintained after the time of Gregory I, during which period the length of the Mass was shortened.

Before the thirteenth century the custom of not repeating the Respond after the verse, if another chant followed such as the Alleluia or the Tract, is seen in a twelfth century ritual of St. Peter's. The repetition occurred in Lent, but only for weekdays if no Tract followed. On other days it was omitted. The Council of Trent sanctioned the performance of the Gradual without repetition at the close, while the repetition in the Introit remained. This circumstance conducted most of all to the suppression of the old name *Responsorium* and the application of " Gradual, " which gives no indication in regard to the form of the piece, for it had lost its responsorial character. Permission for this repeat is given in the 1907 Vatican Gradual. The choir coming in with the soloist at the end of the verse (indicated by a star in the present chant editions) dates from the later Middle Ages. [2]

[1] P. WAGNER, *op. cit.*, p. 84.
[2] *Ibid.*, pp. 88-89.

The Gradual verse is almost always taken from the same book of Holy Scripture as the Gradual, a rule which holds absolutely if the text is taken from the Psalter. The oldest Masses of the *Temporale* have a Psalm Gradual, even as does the *Sanctorale*, and the Masses in which the Gradual text is not taken from the Psalter must be of later origin, [1] a condition which, as we have seen, is the contrary for the Introit Antiphon.

Abandonment of the practice of repeating the Respond at the close of the Psalm verse explains the peculiarities of text or tonality in certain Graduals : the verse of the Gradual *Priúsquam* (1500) ends with the suspended thought : *et díxit míhi*, awaiting the *Priúsquam* and its following text. Wagner states that a manuscript of Leipzig in the Thomas Kirche prescribes the repetition after the verse of this Gradual. [2] We shall see that irregularity between the Respond and verse occurs in the modal sphere as well.

Tonality

Scholarly tabulations in the Apel volume, with additional commentaries, serve for a large part of the statistical and other information contained in the following material on the Gradual modality.

Modal uncertainty occurs less in the Graduals than in the other chants of the Proper. The greater part of the Graduals are written in the four Authentic Modes. However, among this number Mode 5 is used in the greatest abundance, at least one-half of the total. There are about fifty Graduals in Mode 5 contained in the *Liber Usualis*, and about sixty in the Roman Gradual. It is most often combined with its Plagal 6, as in the classic Gradual *Chrístus fáctus est* (655), wherein the Respond is written in Mode 6, while the verse soars up to *g* into the *superabundans* of Mode 5.

Allusion has already been made to the presence of modal irregularities between the Respond and verse. In the Gradual

[1] P. WAGNER, *op. cit.*, pp. 91-92.
[2] *Ibid.*, p. 88.

Ego díxi (found in the Roman Gradual), ascribed to Mode 5, the verse ends on *a*, while the Respond ends on the modal tonic F. The Respond would have to be repeated if the Mode were determined. The presence of the " descending sixth chord " *d-a*-F in the fifth Mode Gradual *Vidérunt ómnes* of the Nativity (409), as well as for about eight Graduals of Mode 8, shows that this progression, rare though it is, belongs to the " old layer of the chant. "

For Mode 1 the *Liber Usualis* contains twelve Graduals, with an additional three in the Roman Gradual. A similarity to Mode 5 occurs in the extended use of standard phrases in the verses, and in the Responds occasional employment especially of short standard phrases. This melodic adaptation and centonization, particularly pronounced in the Gradual verses of Modes 5 and 3, is the result of the soloist's rendition, in order that he might sing with greater ease in memorizing, without so many changes.

The Graduals *Univérsi* (320), *Gloriósus Déus* (1163), and *Adjútor méus* in the Roman Gradual, serve as examples of the combination of Plagal and Authentic Modes 2 and 1 in the Respond and verse respectively. In fact, Wagner ascribes *Gloriósus Déus* to Mode 2.

The Graduals of Mode 2 form a closely unified group. Their number is exceeded only by those of Mode 5. However, about nineteen of these employ the same melody, known as the *Jústus ut pálma* type, of which sixteen are comprised in the *Liber Usualis* and an additional three in the Roman Gradual, apart from the *Haec dies* of the Easter Week days. Willi Apel concludes that the *Jústus ut pálma* type originated in the Mass of Saturday of Ember Week of Advent, in which the four Graduals form a " liturgico-musical nucleus comparable to those of the five Tracts of Holy Saturday. " The first and fourth of this group, *A súmmo caélo* (343) and *Excíte Dómine* (347) contain nearly all the material of the entire group.

The *Haec díes* group (783 ff.), consisting of six Graduals sung in the Easter Sunday Mass and through Friday of Easter Week, together with *Hódie sciétis* (360) and *Técum princípium*

(393), should, in view of their place in the liturgy, be considered as among the oldest Roman chants. More will be said about the *Haec dies* group a little further on.

The Graduals of Mode 3, in common with the *Jústus ut pálma* group, make as full use of standard phrases in their Responds as in their verses, between which in the two latter a close degree of unification exists. These Graduals are generally very long and highly melismatic, as well as centonized. The Graduals of Mode 3 belong mostly to the pre-Easter period, from Septuagesima Sunday, *Adjútor* (498), to Tuesday of Holy Week, *Ego autem* (606).

Mode 4 is sparsely represented among the Graduals. *Tenuísti* (591), from Palm Sunday, the longest of the Graduals, is ascribed to this Mode; but Wagner considers *Ego autem* as also in Mode 4. In *Dómine praevinísti* (1207), ascribed to Mode 4, the verse ends on D in Mode 2, a unique case of a verse employing a different *tonality* in the Respond and verse. Here repetition of the Respond would be imperative if the Mode is established. Apart from the partial adaptation of the melody of *Tenuísti* to *Mémor fúi* (1580), and *Míhi autem*, in the Roman Gradual, as well as the adaptation of *Dómine praevinísti* to *Benedícta et venerábilis* (1264) and *Dolorósa et lacrimósa* (1633$^\text{v}$), no other Graduals are ascribed to Mode 4. With omission of the adaptations, the *Liber Usualis* contains eleven Graduals in Modes 3 and 4, with two more represented in the Roman Gradual.

Mode 7 Graduals are similar to those of Mode 3, through their characteristics of length, melismatic style, and an almost equal amount of centonization in the Respond as well as in the verse. The Gradual *Benedícam* (1028) is particular in that the *Respond* does not end on the modal tonic. Thus repetition of the latter would fail to determine the Mode. The almost unique occurrence in chant of the interval descent of a third and a fifth, is found in the Mode 7 Gradual *Qui sédes* (335), over the word *super*. As Apel points out, the melisma on the word *pácem* of the 7th mode Gradual *Benedíctus Dóminus* (478) is the longest in present day chant. (This refers to the Mass.)

In the same manner in which the Plagal of Mode 5 is incorporated into the Graduals of its Authentic Mode, particularly in the Responds, so is Mode 8 embodied into its allied Mode 7. The former is represented by but two Graduals, namely, *Dilexísti justítiam* (1216) and *Déus vítam méam* in the Roman Gradual. The " triadic design " C-G-E-G-*c*-G in the former Gradual, on the second syllable of *justitiam,* is " indicative of a late date. "

In the Gradual Responds the descending third is about as frequent as the descending second. Ascending motion does not occur in the cadences of the Graduals .[1]

The Gradual *Haec díes* takes its Respond text and all of its verses from Psalm 117 except on Tuesday, on which day it takes it from Psalm 106. Wagner explains this irregularity as follows : " In early times a certain copyist wrote for Easter Sunday the verse *Dícunt nunc qui rédemit,* etc. from Psalm 106 instead of *Dícunt nunc dómus Aáron* from Psalm 117. The error appears as early as the eighth century manuscripts and has survived down to our days. The mistake is explained by the similarity of the verses. These Graduals are all thus connected, and no doubt they formed a single chant with several verses, which was performed on Easter day; later, however, when the Mass Respond was reduced to one verse, it was distributed over the days of Easter Week. " [2]

Adaptation

The process of adaptation and centonization among the Graduals is so profuse that its study could easily comprise a large volume, but examples of these procedures are quite evident to any chant student.

An example of adaptation of one chant to another text is found, among others, in the melody of 1) *Chrístus fáctus*

---

[1] In the order in which it appears, the foregoing matter which has been borrowed from Apel's *Gregorian chant* is as follows : 168, 254, 350, 351, 352, 358, 138, 362, 360, 355, 354, 255, 158, 357, 264.

[2] P. WAGNER, *op. cit.*, p. 90.

est (655) to 2) *Exiit sérmo* (422), of the Feast of St. John, Apostle and Evangelist. The tonic accent in each initial word is strongly supported with the same *pressus*. The following phrase in each piece contains six syllables. The tonic accents in each are similarly ornamented, with a variant of 1 for the first composite neum on *frátres* in 2, both settings equally satisfying. The tonic accents of the two significant words, *obédiens* of 1 and *discípulus* of 2, are highlighted with an inspiring melisma which transcends the Plagal Mode setting of the Respond, and concludes on the following syllables of the same words.

A striking motif is that of the prolonged F for the tonic accent of the word *crúcis* of 1 and *móritur* of 2, moving symbolically downward on the last syllable of each of these two key-words, both followed by the same artistically developed cadence.

One of the most uplifting passages in Gregorian Chant, soaring up to the summit of the highest Mode, *g*, follows the word *íllum* in the verse of 1. The word *exaltávit* which immediately precedes, signals the advent of this exhilarating *jubilus* of exaltation. In 2 this melisma is reserved for the meaningful word *manére*, but its soaring contour is more in keeping with the sentiment of 1 at this place.

From here on the text in 1 is five syllables in excess of that of 2, which, except for a short motif of similarity which follows the long melisma, results in diverse settings until they meet at the developed final cadence. *Chrístus fáctus est* is a magnificent song of triumph over death.

It is to be noticed that in chant so highly melismatic in parts as that just examined, the song writer's fine sense of relation never permits him to set a long melisma on tonic accents, while leaving the unaccented syllables of the word comparatively bare. The ornamental motives on even the unaccented syllables at times serve not to enhance these syllables as such, but to portray the textual significance of the word as a whole, be it one of joy or one of sorrow, of an uplifting or of a depressing nature.

While still on the subject of adaptation of the Gradual, it is significant to observe the melodic setting of the same verbal text for two dissimilar songs, the Introit Antiphon *Hódie sciétis* (359) of Christmas Eve, and the Gradual Respond (360) of the same Mass. Each piece with its individual style retains like conservation of verbal importance, with due proportion in the melody as well.

Melodic Procedures for Expressive and Symbolic Elements

In the verse of the Gradual *Omnes de Sába* of the Epiphany (459), the opening word *Súrge* is melodically portrayed in a manner that depicts the vehemence with which the prophet uttered this command. The repeated motif for the two cadences of this word could signify his *insistance* that Jerusalem *arise* and be *enlightened*, for the " glory of the Lord is risen " upon her. The tonic accent of the word *illumináre* opens up on a mounting melisma that penetrates to the point of purest melodic light, *f*, summit of the Mode — dramatic procedures of the greatest virility.

It has already been pointed out, in study of the Offertory *Impropérium* (600), that it is not the importance of a word by itself that determines its significance in the text, but it is the modifying influence which this word expresses in the entire subject matter that gives it a particular expressive quality. For example, in the Gradual Respond *Adjútor in opportunitátibus* (498), again with the monosyllable *non*, but here with different significance, the psalmist gives vent to all his feelings of trust that God forsakes *not* those who seek Him. Accordingly, no word in the Respond is so highly ornamented as this diminutive term. In addition, the modal dominant *c* fashioned in various rhythmic patterns highlights this negative in impressive fashion.

In the verse the song writer has gone to even greater length to bring out the importance of this little word. Starting in an elevated range, as at its first appearance, the melody climbs still higher after its first cadence on *b*, original modal dominant, where it springs a fourth to the summit of the Mode; then still higher to *f*, whence it descends on the inverted diminished triad *f-d-b*, only to rise again for the following inverted minor traid *e-c-a*, then back again to *c*, which with its dominant play and prolongation continues to enhance the powerful meaning of this little monosyllable as a symbol of the unswerving confidence of the persistently ardent and struggling soul. Likewise, the aspiring motif on the tonic accent of the word *páuperum*, rounding off on the following syllables with well-proportioned neums, sheds added light regarding those to whose prayers God never turns a deaf ear — the poor of spirit.

The cry *exsúrge* is brought out with a sudden symbolic spring of a fourth on its tonic accent, followed by inversion of the same wide interval on the atonic syllable. The melody then remains in the upper range of intense imploration, and descends only at the cadence which precedes the word *hómo*. From here the melody works up through a double *podatus*, again to the dominant, and continues with a series of neums adapted in contrary movement, all fashioned together in broad arsic and thetic lines. The final cadence of the song takes a further swing up to the dominant *c* before settling on the modal tonic, that which to the end stamps this cry of faith in Him by whom " the needy shall *not* always be forgotten, for the patience of the poor shall not perish. "

In the verse of the Gradual *Tribulatiónes córdis* (546) a striking melodic procedure is employed on the tonic accent of the word *labórum*. During the course of a long melisma a twice-repeated descending double interval drop, consisting of a major fourth and a major third, *d-a-F*, accord outstanding dynamic importance to the labor which the psalmist insists the Lord should regard as well as his humility, that He may remove his sin and end his affliction. A similar procedure is used in the Gradual *Bónum est confídere* (1037) on the word *est*, but more dramatically in the formerly sung Gradual *Propter veritátem* (1062) on the tonic accent of the word *fília* after the command " Audi ," that which accords forceful persistence to the word *fília*, making it imperative that " the daughter hear and turn her ear, for the King has greatly desired her beauty. " As further example, the same motif occurs again on the final syllable of the word *Láqueus* in the Gradual *Anima nóstra* (1167).

The *gamma*, G, inferior note to the lowest modal tonic which owes its name to St. Odo of Cluny (d. 942), is used in forceful manner at six places in the formerly sung Palm Sunday Responsory *Collegérunt Pontífices* (579). It occurs in seven more pieces in the *Liber usualis* and also in the verses of two Offertories. The use of this low note in *Collegérunt* shows the limits to which the song writer went to portray the debased, sinister motives of the chief priests and council of the Jews. At *Quid fácimus* there is a sudden departure from the previous scale intervals. These words emerge on the upward unprepared spring of a fifth followed by its immediate inversion. Through this abrupt melodic procedure one actually *hears* the emotional consternation of the conspirators as they ask one another in agitated tones how they are going to rid themselves of " the man who is working many signs. " After the word *signa* the melody drops for the fourth time to the *gamma* for a neumatic octave-run on the tonic accent of *fécit*. It occurs again on the words *illíus* and *prophetávit*, as though Caiphus himself were also under the spell of his dark environment until his words of prophecy take form despite himself. With this latter utterance the melody ascends into the region of declamation.

The climax occurs with the final sentence. For this an impressive delivery is prepared by means of an extended melisma on the preposition *ab*, which acts as a sort of prelude to revelation of the plan for execution of the most ominous crime in history — Crucifixion of the Creator of Heaven and Earth!

Note that in a liturgical Respond other than the Gradual, the repeat of the latter part of the Respond after the verse is obligatory.

One of the many beautifully wrought Gradual verse cadences bears analysis. The Gradual *Benedícam Dóminum* (1028) can serve as an example of this skill. This long melismatic cadence starts with a composite neum ending with a *pressus* that resolves on *c*, dominant of the Plagal Mode. This motif is then repeated and the *pressus* resolves on *d*, dominant of the Authentic Mode. A *distropha* with *pressus* of *f* follows, then a portion of the original motif without the *pressus* resolves on *b*, after which three triple-note neums in varied setting, the third and final ending in a *pressus*, carry this well-woven vocalization to G, its tonic note of rest.

A further symbolic melisma which soars to the heights is seen in the Gradual *Dirigátur orátio méa* (1060). On the tonic accent of the word *elevátio* an unusual melodic rise to *a*, a degree beyond the summit of the highest Mode, carries the melody to the most elevated regions, after which it descends in contrary movement to the cadence, where a further rise mounts to the upper modal tonic before resolving on the dominant at the close of the word.

In the Gradual *Communicántes* (1482) the tonic accent of the key-word *gaudéte* is ornamented with a three-fold composite neum, each comprising a *pressus*. This persistent repetition of the same intensive melodic figure draws sharp attention to the supernatural gift of joy while partaking of the sufferings of Christ.

A paragraph at the close of the section devoted to the Graduals in the Willi Apel opus, already referred to in this study, is too impressive to forego quoting in its original. The author first quotes Peter Wagner's estimate of the Gradual melodies at the end of the latter's portrayal of the same : " It is possible to gather gems which, considered individually, delight us by their cut, brilliance and rareness; if, however, they are to form a precious piece of jewelry, they must receive a splendid mounting, an ingenious connection, and a tasteful arrangement Are the old melodies combined in this manner? " Apel himself continues : " Wagner's answer is, of course, in the positive, and no one will hesitate to concur with him to the fullest extent. These melodies, fascinating in their analytical detail, are equally admirable for their synthetic quality, for their cohesion and union. In fact, the perception of their structural properties greatly enhances their significance as unified works of art, no less so than in a Sonata of Beethoven. True enough, there is the difference that in Beethoven the analytical details occur within one individual work, whereas in Gregorian Chant they appear only upon comparison of a sufficient number of different

113

pieces. To state this is only to emphasize once more, and demonstrate with special clarity, that a Gregorian melody is not an individual creation but representative of a type. " [1]

Certainly one of the most remarkable added features of liturgical plainchant is its melodic and rhythmic variety all obtained virtually within the radius of less than an octave of notes, without chromatic alterations, harmonic modulations, or varied note measurement. That any music as stimulating as Gregorian Chant could be effected within the bounds of the limited melodic material that it is, proves the peculiar aptitude possessed by these early artisans for creating a song of such beauty, virility and inspiration that it has held its own without peer for some sixteen centuries in the life of Christendom.

ALLELUIA

History

The second responsorial song of the Mass is likewise an inheritance from the Jewish liturgy. Its prototype existed in the Temple of Solomon and continued to be used in the Synagogue as a liturgical acclamation or refrain to the Psalm verses chanted by the soloist. The word " allelúia " is derived from the imperative plural of the Hebrew word *hillel* (to praise), *hallelu + yah* (abbreviation of Yahweh). The Church continued to use this ejaculation in Hebrew just as she did the terms " Amen, " " Hosanna " and others, even though they could have been translated into the prevailing language, in order to preserve unchanged certain traditional customs.

" Alleluia " was one of the popular ejaculations of the early Church. This Hebrew acclamation, modulated on all forms, became the refrain of gladness which accompanied the daily occupations of the peaceful populations converted to the faith. It was the Christian's cry of victory emerging from two and a half centuries of persecution and oppression, and in reunions of the cult was the most frequently used of the musical

[1] W. Apel, *op. cit.*, p. 362.

114

acclamations by which the entire assembly united in the chant of the Church. Sailors at sea saluted one another from afar with the cry " Allelúia! " Rowers used it for the cadence of the refrain of a canticle which they sang to Christ. Venerable Bede (d. 735) recounts that St. Germain, Bishop of Auxerre (5th c.), commanded the soldiers to sing it before battle, so that with this cry they might march to combat and win victory without bloodshed.

The Allelúia, especially with its character of refrain sung by the people, constitutes one of the most venerable and the most ancient representations of the sung prayer of the Mass during the first ages of Christianity. St. Jerome testifies to the Allelúia sung by the people as a refrain to the soloist's Psalm verses sung at the Sunday Mass. St. Augustine speaks several times of the Allelúia of Pentecost as an ancient tradition of the Church heard everywhere during the fifty days after Easter.

Just prior to Gregory's time the Allelúia would seem to have been sung only during Eastertide. This association with Easter, unknown to the East where they sing the Allelúia always, even in Offices of the Dead, as was once done in Rome, afterwards led to adoption of further Allelúias incorporated into other pieces of the Mass: Introit, Offertory, Communion, etc., especially during Eastertide. St. Gregory extended use of the Allelúia to all Sundays and feast days.

Although liturgically and textually the early Allelúias go back to the time of Gregory, this is not necessarily the case as regards their melodies. Many Allelúias were written in the eighth century. In fact, their composition continues up to the fifteenth century, the only chant of the Mass proper for which texts and melodies were written until such a late epoch.

Form

In the early Church the Allelúia, as already stated, was sung by the people as a refrain to the Psalm verses, and probably in simple syllabic setting. At its origin it accompanied an entire Psalm, as in the early form of the Gradual.

Both the East and the West used the Allelúia song before the Gospel prior to the fourteenth century. The Allelúia's place before the Gospel is peculiar to the Roman rite. In the Gallican rite it is sung after the Gospel, and this is now also the custom in the Orient.

Participation of the people in rendition of the Allelúia ceased around the middle of the fifth century, at about the same time that they relinquished their singing of the first responsorial song of the Mass, the Gradual. In the history of the latter it was seen that during the fifth century the three initial readings of the Mass, Prophecy, Epistle, Gospel, were reduced to the two latter, but the Psalms remained two as independant pieces between the Epistle and Gospel. The first of the two Psalms was reduced to the two parts of the Gradual, and from the second the single verse of the Allelúia resulted. The soloist of the Allelúia stood on the lower step of the ambo, as was the case for the chanter of the Gradual, and turned toward the East.

According to the testimony of Augustine and Cassiodorus (d. 580), it is probable that the Allelúia *jubilus* of the pre-Gregorian Mass, as sung by the soloist, was a very extended melody. It cannot be said with certainty at what point it became the custom to use one or more Psalm verses in the later developed Allelúia. According to some sources it was not until the time of Gregory, but at all events it was sometime between 530-750. Wagner's opinion is that St. Gregory, in appointing this chant as a regular constituent part of the Mass determined the particular Psalm verses to be used in the Roman Mass, but the choice of these Psalm verses in other countries of the Roman liturgy was left open. The added words to the Alleluia *júbili* were necessitated by the elaborate musical character of the pre-Gregorian Allelúias. The reviser of the liturgy must have considered these *júbili* so rich in melismatic beauty that he would not shorten them, but he managed by adding Psalm verses to give them a better liturgical form, without cutting down the richness of the melody [1].

[1] P. WAGNER, *op. cit.*, pp. 93, 94, 96.

Wagner further states that in the Allelúia, unlike the Gradual, the repetition after each verse remained in use during all the Middle Ages, as has continued to be the case for the repeated Allelúia after the verse, so that even today the Allelúia is a genuine responsonal chant in form. Deviations from this general rule are to be found in the Allelúia *Confitémini* (759) of Holy Saturday, but probably because the Tract *Laudáte Dóminum ómnes géntes* follows immediately. This manner of performance was afterwards adopted for similar Allelúias, as for the Allelúia of the Greater Litanies of the same text (841), although here no chant follows immediately but instead the Gospel. However, the repetition must have taken place on these days, as an old *Ordinarium* still directs this expressly. The Tridentine Missal has established as general rule the now prevailing custom of the Middle Ages. The Commission also struck out more than one verse [1].

The Allelúia is thus the only chant of the Mass Proper that has retained classic responsorial form to the present day: A-A-B-A.

It is also a later arrangement that the Gradual Responds are supplanted by a second Allelúia during Eastertide. However, in Easter Week itself the Gradual is retained before the Allelúia. The Ember Saturday after Pentecost has five Allelúias instead of the normal sequence of four Graduals and a Hymn for the Saturdays of Ember Week. The five Allelúias replaced the five or six Graduals used until the eleventh or twelfth centuries.

The late Allelúias of the fourteenth and fifteenth centuries are new in text and melody. Wagner considers them a decay in liturgical composition in their systematic rejection of prayers from the Bible, especially the Psalter. In some cases fragments of Christian poems are used or other verses not taken from the Bible. Melodically these late Allelúias show a tendency for modern tonality, especially Mode 5. [2] (See *Assúmpta est* 1603, *Beátus vir* 1747, etc.)

---

[1] P. WAGNER, *op. cit.*, pp. 95, 97.

[2] *Ibid.*, p. 98.

The Allelúia verse *Vírgo Déi Génetrix* (1684) is metrical. Ferretti calls the Allelúia verses *Fac nos* (1441) and *Sólve* (1576) also metrical. Willi Apel points out an interesting feature in the Allelúia verse *Scitóte quóniam* (1296) in the use of two consecutive descending fourths, *c*-G-D, on the word *ípsi*, the only example of this formation in present-day chant editions. [1]

Tonality

All eight Modes are contained in the Allelúias. However, Modes 1 and 2 and 7 and 8 are the most frequently employed, with Modes 5 and 6 least, a contrast to the Graduals. The least represented is the last Mode, used for Allelúia *Dómine in virtúte* in the *Liber Usualis* (1003) and for *Magníficat* for the Feast of the Immaculate Heart of Mary (a recent feast), *Dóminus dábit vérbum* for the Feast of St. John Francis Regis, and *Condémnat* for the Feast of St. John Berchmans, the last two contained in the Roman Gradual in the section " for other places. "

Authentic and Plagal Modes intermingle between the Allelúia with its *jubilus* and the verse. Mixture of Modes also occurs : the *Allelúia* and *jubilus* of *Véni Dómine* (354) are in Mode 3, but the verse is entirely in Modes 1 and 2, strongly established with a modal cadence on D. The repeated *allelúia* and *jubilus* return to the original Mode. The same melody is used for *Paráta cor méum* (1064) and *Adducéntur* (1217).

Adaptation

For a synthetic tabulation of the Allelúias in their unique form of adaptation, we again draw upon an Apel summation. The following " repeat types " constitute a partial list of descriptive forms extracted virtually from the aforenamed author's work *Gregorian Chant* :

1) A restatement of the entire first section at the end of the verse, of which there are about sixty cases, relatively rare in Mode 7, but very frequent in Mode 1. (See *Surréxit*

[1] W. APEL, *op. cit.*, p. 256.

Dóminus, 790, *Christus resúrgens*, 827, *Nos vos relínquam*, 856.)
2) Only the jubilus is repeated at the end of the verse, but the melisma is slightly shortened. (See *Páscha nóstrum*, 779, and *Adorábo*, 1251). In some cases the melisma is expanded. (See *Te décet hýmnus*, 1022.) At times the melodic material which precedes repetition of the *jubilus* at the end of the verse, is borrowed from the *Allelúia*, but is not a full repetition of the *Allelúia* melody. (See *Sápentia hújus*, 1428).

3) The verse starts with the *Allelúia* melody, then goes into new melodic material until the end of the verse, where the *Allelúia* melody reappears, followed by the *jubilus*. (See *Quínque prudéntes*, 1339.)

4) The *Allelúia* melody reappears at the beginning of the verse, followed by new material. It reappears during the course of the verse again followed by new material, while the *jubilus* alone is used for the close of the verse. (See *Exsultáte Déo*, 1026.)

5) The verse starts with the *Allelúia* melody, but neither this nor the *jubilus* are used at the close of the verse. (See *Quóniam Déus*, 1042, a unique example.)

6) The *Allelúia* melody occurs at the beginning of the verse, followed by the first part of the *jubilus*, and is used again at the end followed by the *jubilus* in its entirely. (See *Dispérsit*, 1480.)

7) The *Allelúia* melody and its *jubilus* occur twice at the close of the verse. (See *Ego sum pástor*, 818.)

8) The verse consists entirely of a double setting of the *Allelúia* melody and the *jubilus*. (See *Spíritus éjus*, 902.) [1]

Repetition of motives during the course of the *jubilus* is also very prominent in the Allelúia song. As examples, in *Véni Dómine* (354) there is immediate repetition of the first part of the *jubilus*, and a repeated motif in the verse on the tonic accent of *facínora*. The same procedures occur in the *jubilus* and verse of *Parátum cor méum* (1064). The repeat in the verse

---

[1] W. APEL, *op. cit.*, pp. 384-385.

is on the tonic accent of the word *glória*, a melody we have already seen in the section on Tonality. Especially effective is the repeat of the motif including the broken seventh on the expressive word *mors* in the verse of *Christus resúrgens* (827).

Adaptation is a pronounced trait of the Alleluia song, but centonization is not one of its features. According to Wagner, one-third, or about seventy Allelúias in present-day use are adaptations. There are scarcely more than ten Allelúias in which the verse has no relation to the Allelúia section. But, Apel adds, the distinguishing feature in the Allelúias is not that its adaptations are in greater quantity than the remaining chants of the Mass Proper, but that they occur in Masses of such early date, while in other chants they are found only for feasts of a later date. As portrayed above, uniformity among the Allelúias consists essentially in analogous aspects of form and structure, while at the same time each song retains its individual character, a particularity of the Offertory as well. This condition Apel calls freedom " from bondage to liberty. "

Wagner considers that absence of the *jubilus* in repeat form at the end of the verse, among which are included the three Masses of the Nativity (394, 405, 409), is in general an indication that the song is more archaic, before the sense of symmetry was established. On the other hand, Apel is of the opinion that particular characteristics such as small range and absence of repeated melismata offer a more satisfying basis for the period of composition than does the aspect of a repeated *jubilus* at the end of the verse. [1]

The largest group of complete song adaptation is that of the third Mass of the Nativity, *Dies sanctificátus* (409). Wagner considers this text a translation of the Greek original. Adaptations of the Latin text are excellently coordinated, as is evident in the following examples : 1) *Dies sanctificátus* to 2) *Video caélos* (416), 3) *Hic est discipúlis* (422), 4) *Vidimus stéllam* (460).

In all four settings the first and tonically accented syllable of the verse is fortified by the uplifting melisma that prepares

---

[1] W. APEL, *op. cit.*, pp. 381, 383, 384, 385, 391.

the spirit of praise the term "allelúia" conveys. The second developed melisma is on the tonic accent of 1) *nóbis,* 2) *apértos,* 3) *ílle,* 4) *éjus.* In 1 the tonic accent of *veníte,* with its double descending *pressus* on D followed by a major fourth drop on the same note, portrays a melodic insistance that bodes no refusal by the nations that they come to adore the Lord whose great Light has descended upon the earth this day. In rendition each simple neum in this composite one should be expressed with increased augmented arsic intensity. In 2 this expressive motif falls on the tonic accent of *stántem,* in 3 on the breve syllable of *pérhibet,* and in 4 on the tonic accent of the key-word *Oriénte.*

The tonic accent of the key-word in 1, *hódie,* receives a dynamic *salicus,* followed by strong composite neums for its following syllables. This motif fits in perfectly for the word *déxtris* of 2, the significant word *scímus* of 3, and *vénimus* of 4. The *greatness* of the Light which has descended upon the earth is admirably portrayed by the undulating vocalization which unfolds on the tonic accent of *mágna* in 1, resolving on a simple *punctum* for the atonic syllable, which, with its tonal cadence prolongation gives due proportion to the word as a whole.

Except for the *c* used as an appoggiatura at the first cadence of *mágna,* the notes which comprise this first part of the vocalization are the same as those employed for the entire motif of *hódie.* It is enlightening to observe the variety of rhythm the song writer has effected between the two sets of the same five notes.

The entire melismatic adornment of *mágna* is reserved for the tonic accent of the equally important words *virtútis* of 2, *vérum* of 3, and the significant word *munéribus* of 4. Except for an opening *distropha* in 2, the closing cadence of 1 is applied in like setting to the spondaic words of 2 and 3, with a repeated note for the dactyl of 4.

A further noteworthy adaptation is that of the Allelúia verse 1) *Jústi epuléntur* (1168) to 2) *Ego vos elégi* (1487). With exception of a preceding *punctum* and the motif for the word *Déi* and that of the first two syllables of *delecténtur,* both in 1, and the melodic phrase for *et frúctum* through inclusion of the

121

following *et* of 2, the longer text, the melody and tonically accented words of both versions coincide. The tonic accents of the three significant words of 1, *epuléntur*, *delecténtur* and *laetítia*, are adorned with highly developed melismata, applied respectively to the tonic accents of *elégi*, *frúctus* and *máneat* of 2. This long vocalization for the word *delecténtur* of 1 and for *frúctus* of 2, comprises a rising seventh made up of a major fifth and a minor third, a dynamic setting which highlights both words, the *delight* of the just, and the *fruit* of the Apostles, for it is indeed by this that " they shall be known. " And if the fruits of those whom the Lord has chosen did not *remain*, as this Gospel text stresses, there would be but a transitory character to their value instead of an eternal one.

Melodic Procedures for Expressive and Symbolic Elements

As in all the chant pieces studied thus far, the Allelúia is no exception to the expressive and dramatic elements embodied in the texts of its song and preserved through melodic procedures of great ingenuity.

The ecstatic melisma on the tonic accent of the climactic word *immolátus* in the Easter Sunday Allelúia *Páscha nóstrum* (779) rises to *a*, transcending the highest of all modal notes. This already developed vocalization is repeated for reinforcement and is then followed by long arsic and thetic melodic waves which gradually descend to the modal tonic G on a two-fold cadence. This exceptionally extended jubilation gives the impression of a desire to go on eternally proclaiming the victorius means of redemption chosen for the immolated Victim of the Passion. For length it is a close second to the melisma already pointed out in the Gradual *Benedíctus Dóminus*.

In the Allelúia verse *Angelus Dómini* (786) one not only hears but actually *sees* the rolling melody that falls down in a cascade of triple *torculi* on the tonic accent of the word *revólvit*, as the Angel of the Lord rolls back the stone. Willi Apel questions the validity of this interpretation for the revolving figure, on the grounds that it is not indicated in the neumatic notation of manuscript 359 of St. Gall. He concludes that it is an innovation of the tenth or eleventh century. [1] This might well be the case, since symbolism played a decided role in the Church arts of the Middle Ages, starting about the eleventh century. It would seem highly felicitous that these later editions of Church music might also have benefited from this expressive element.

But why should we chide a possible later scribe for enhancing a text with an appropriate small ornamental figure which but adds to its significance, when the ornamental figures of Bach, Mozart and Beethoven are also given diverse interpretations of the manuscripts by music editors? The ultimate orthodoxy of an " editorial modification " in liturgical chant, as in all expressions of music, would seem to rest principally on the degree of the modification, that it remain in harmonious accord with the original, and that it add to the interpretive value of the text in so doing. Besides, there is also disagreement in the old chant manuscripts in small particulars such as this.

The fruits of the Passion let themselves be known in one word — Redemption. For which reason the most expressively ornamented word in the Allelúia *Surréxit Chrístus et illúxit* (831) is *redémit*. Its tonic accent climbs to the summit of the Mode, *d*, in its only appearance in the verse, followed by a series of neums adapted in contrary movement, resolving on the modal dominant *a*. The persistent double *pressus* followed by a composite neum on the tonic accent of *sánguine*, all in lower melodic setting, leaves no doubt regarding the *means* by which redemption is bought — the shedding of blood.

In the Allelúia verse *Non vos relínquam* (856) abundantly ornamented melismata highlight the tonic accent of the key-word *gaudébit*. The interspersed fivefold *clivis* in the first melisma, followed by a repeated rising fourth in the second one, leading up to a series of neums in singable scale intervals, symbolize the profound import of this word. For after Christ had divulged to the eleven that He must leave them and go to the Father,

[1] W. APEL, *op. cit.*, p. 303.

He saw that it was too much for them to bear. As He gazes on the dejected countenances about Him compassion fills His heart. Suddenly His voice changes from one of quiet discourse to one of hope, as, in reassuring tones, He promises that He will not leave them orphans. A contagious element of joy rings out in His voice as He prophecies that their hearts will *rejoice*, because after He has gone He will return to them. Note the symbolic melodic ascent on *vádo* and descent on *vénio*.

The final cadence of a triple *podatus* of a rising fifth, followed by melismata augmentation with intensity for each repetition, a repetition of the *jubilus*, give the ultimate seal to the infallible promise just made.

A dynamic and not infrequent procedure is employed in the Allelúia verse of the new (1929) Mass of the Sacred Heart, *Tollíte júgum méum* (972). Starting at the second *et* a rising seventh is effected through the sequence of a major fourth and a minor third. This in turn is followed by a *climacus* in *pressus* form from the summit of the seventh, rounded off with a *clivis* and a *podatus*. Fur the sake of emphasis the entire motif is repeated. The proclamatory nature of this motif with its repetition acts as a sort of prelude to the significant words *húmilis Córde*, each of whose tonic accents is supported with a *pressus* in a composite neum. The motif of *et*, used singly, is repeated for the tonic accent of *réquiem*, with an added cadence, thus reinforcing the result of " humility of heart, — the gift of peace. "

An interval process similar to the one just described occurs on the tonic accent of the key-word *Pretiósa* in the Allelúia verse of that name (1151). But here the rise of a seventh is effected through the sequence of two direct major fourths. In rendition an element of special arsic impulse should be accorded the first note of each of the two simple neums comprising the seventh. With this more unusual melodic procedure for the first and expressive word of the verse, the song writer interprets in song the psalmist's ode : " In the eyes of God the death of His holy martyrs is as *precious* as gold which has been proved in a furnace. "

In *Te Mártyrum* (1171) a procedure more in keeping with later chant composition, six diatonic notes in scale progression, is used for the first two syllables of the word *Allelúia*, as well as in repeated form at the close of the *jubilus* and verse. This figure combines a triple *podatus*, the last of which rounds off on a *pressus*. In measured music these six scale notes would be interpreted in note-by-note *crescendo*. In free rhythm, on the contrary, they are interpreted as three two-note rhythmic units. In rendition, an arsic impulse is accorded the first note of each of these units, most to the secondary accent of the word *Allelúia*, least to the first neum of the breve syllable, with an intermediary quantity for the third *podatus* but followed by an augmented expansion on the *pressus* combined with it. One of Notker's Sequences, *Laus tíbi Chrísti*, is an adaptation of the melody of this *Allelúia*.

A further example of artistry is seen in the *jubilus* of the Allelúia *Qui séquitur me* (1139), where the melody moves in contrasting intervals of rises and falls up to the cadence, in traversing the full extension of the modal gamut. Particularly interesting is the A-C-D-F ascension of two minor thirds.

A skillfull and artistic *jubilus* for the Allelúia *Tóta púlchra es* (1318) offers an example of interesting effects with simple means : an identical motif is employed for each of the three final cadences. The first and second are interspersed with a mounting motif which starts like the cadence figures, but which transcends them by the interval of a fourth, followed by a composite neum which runs in contrary movement. The second and third cadences are also separated by a composite neum in contrary movement, but arranged in opposite directions from the first interspersed motif. Through this ingenious treatment of the varied interpolations, the triple delivery of the three like cadences is not only shorn of all element of tiresome uniformity, but, on the contrary, is transformed into little melodic units, which, through their very repetition, become ever more satisfying. This *jubilus* has the allure of a little folk song. Dom Johner tells us that the melody of this Allelúia was originally sung on the Feasts of the Assumption and St. Agnes.

Something in the nature of the *jubilus* just described occurs at the final cadence of the Allelúia verse *Qui ad justítiam* (1467). This cadence incorporates the same twice repeated *torculus*, the first and second followed by the same *clivis*, the third followed by a *clivis* which rises one degree higher than the two preceding ones, lending a touch of variety at just the right place — further instance of aesthetic effect produced with the simplest of procedures.

The verse of the Allelúia *Quinque prudéntes* (1339) brings this series to a close. A most dramatic melisma sets off the climactic word *clámor*, as we have also seen this word particularized in the Communion of the same text. In the Allelúia verse full melodic vent is given to its expressive significance. This extended melisma comprises a repeated motif with a *pressus* on *f*, summit of the melody, followed by a *climacus resupinus*. The repetition is followed in turn by a descending composite neum including a *pressus*, all in hexachord scale intervals, leading into a cadence on the modal tonic.

TRACT

History

The third manner of delivery in liturgical song is likewise adapted from Jewish custom. It consists of the singing of a Psalm from one end to the other, repeating nothing and intercalating nothing. This chant may be on one or on several tones. The Tract (L. *tractim*, straightway) of the Mass exemplifies this manner of execution. Whether it be varied in modulation or whether it be sung alternately by two choirs or by solo and choir, it is nevertheless *in uno tractu* (going straight along) in its manner of delivery. The term *in uno tractu* belongs to the idea of the way in which a text is combined and not to any special variants in its melodic intervals. The Tracts go back to the eulogies connected with the prophetic lessons of the Synanogue. [1] It can furthermore be demonstrated that

---

[1] E. WERNER, *op. cit.*, p. 6.

the entire structure of the liturgy of Holy Saturday was constituted of elements of the Day of Atonement and the Feast of Passover combined. The lessons show that most clearly *(id.)*.

The oldest chant books contain Tracts only for the Sundays from Septuagesima to Psalm Sunday, for Ash Wednesday, Friday and Saturday of Holy Week, and also for the feasts of those saints which usually fall within this season. Thus the eighth century Gradual of Monza has for the Feast of St. Valentine the Tract *Desidérium* (1131), and of St. Felix, Priest and Martyr, *Beátus vir* commemorated January 14 (1394). Later it was the custom to sing the Tract also on week days of Lent. However, in this case nothing was composed, but the existing material was made to serve. [1]

Form

Originally a whole Psalm was sung, but eventually it became shortened to two or three verses. Psalm 116, sung Saturday of Ember Week of Lent and at Lauds of Holy Saturday, is the shortest of the Tracts with a full Psalm, but two verses. Each verse of a Tract is marked V., except the beginning verse, but which is also a part of the Psalm verses, calling attention to its nature as a solo chant sung straight through without interpolation by the choir.

There are still a few Masses where the Tract has virtually kept its original nature as a whole Psalm : the first Sunday of Lent, Palm Sunday (the longest Tract), Good Friday, all in Mode 2. The Tract text is nearly always taken from Holy Scripture, but at times from books other than the Psalter. (See *Cantémus Dómino*, 745, *Gáude María Vírgo*, 1266, *Te Déum Pátrem*, 1273, etc.). Some of the verses used consecutively are taken from various Psalms with a common sentiment of text. (See *Dómine non secúndum*, 527 : Psalm 102, 10; 78, 8, 9).

The Tract represents the oldest form of solo psalmody sung during the Mass. In the ancient liturgy the lector sang the Canticles and executed the Tract intercalated between the

---

[1] P. WAGNER, *op. cit.*, pp. 100-101.

scriptural readings. The first Roman ordo shows that it was sung from the steps of the ambo, like the Gradual. According to the third Roman ordo the cantor of the Tract of the Alleluia is to be a different person from the cantor of the Gradual. What was solo came to be sung by the whole choir. The form remained the same but the execution changed.

Wagner states that the length of the Tract is proof of its great antiquity. He is inclined to believe that the Tracts of the medieval manuscripts exhibit the last remnants of the original Gradual Psalms. Its present form must be that which belonged to all responsorial Psalms before the abbreviation. He demonstrates how the Tracts *Dómine exáudi* (614) and *Dómine audívi* (695) are really responsories (the latter so-titled in today's liturgy), for in the old manuscripts they preserve the repetitions that are characteristic of responsories, and which the Tract never had. They were not sung *in directum*, but with the first verse repeated. They were called *Graduale* or *Responsorium* in the oldest manuscripts and have been called Tracts only since the tenth century, at which time the repeat of the first verse was omitted. Both chants were called Tracts only because in the Proper the Gradual had at that time lost all but one of its verses, and those being longer seemed to bear a likeness to the Tract. [1]

The Antiphonary of Monza (8th. c.) calls the Gradual *Beáta Gens* (1048) also a Tract. These Tracts are properly responsories, Wagner adds, and all those which use the same melody or its motif in the manuscripts and printed books are only in an improper sense called Tracts — that is all the Tracts of Mode 2. In their structure and manner of performance they are Gradual Responds, and in them is preserved a valuable relic of the early medieval manner of singing, for here, as in general, Lent proves to be very rich in ancient tradition. [2]

It is probable, Wagner goes on to say, that the Tract melodies are extremely old and venerable monuments of the chant of

[1] P. WAGNER, *op. cit.*, pp. 89, 99, 100.
[2] *Ibid.*, p. 90.

128

the Latin Church, and they preserve the *melodic form of the solo psalmody* of the Mass in the shape in which they were used *up to the fourth and fifth centuries* in Italy, when the solo singers began to deck them with richer melismata than before, and by this innovation brought on the abbreviation of the Psalm. This suggestion is especially borne out by the fact that far into the Middle Ages all the texts of the Tracts without exception came from the Psalter or the Biblical Canticles. When the Gradual Psalms were shortened the forms of the original Gradual psalmody were prescribed for penitential seasons only. [1]

Most of the Tracts are derived from one or two musical themes, the *hirmos,* a model theme from which the remaining ones developed. Each Tract consists almost completely of a succession of standard pieces. The melody was written at the head of the long text to which the various sections were sung. The general construction of the Tract conforms to the following plan : a) The first melody of the Tract begins with a characteristic formula; b) The last verse closes with a long formula, a melismatic coda; c) The dominant is used as tenor throughout the song; d) Every verse contains more than one mediant cadence.

The Tracts are highly melismatic, on the order of the Gradual. Willi Apel assumes that the final form of the Tract was the result of an embellishing process in the Franco-Germanic lands of the eighth century. [2]

The Tract is sung on all days of penance, which means that the Allelúia is omitted on those days. Like the latter, its function is a more ornamental one in the liturgy in contrast to the Gradual, whose role, as previously stated, is a purely liturgical one.

Tonality

All the Tracts are in Modes 2 and 8. The latter group are probably the more ancient, but the longest Tracts are in

[1] P. WAGNER, *op. cit.,* p. 100.

[2] W. APEL, *op. cit.,* p. 511.

Mode 2. In fact, they are the longest songs in Gregorian Chant. These two Modes demonstrate the archaic period when the Modes were not yet determined.

Adaptation and Centonization

Adaptation of like musical formulae in different Tracts is so characteristic of this chant of the Proper, that in this realm there is comparatively little that is not an example of this procedure. For example, the five Mode 8 Tracts of Holy Saturday are all of the same design, a condition already pointed out as comparable to the four Mode 2 Graduals of the Saturday Mass of Ember Week of Advent, in which two Graduals contain the material of the entire group. [1]

The first of the Holy Saturday Tracts, *Cantémus Dómino* (745) is now sung after the reading of the first and second Lessons, and is titled " Canticle. " Its text is taken from the Canticle of Moses. In comparison of this setting, 1) with that of 2) *Qui confídunt* (561) of the fourth Sunday of Lent, the following similarities and differences may be cited :

Both songs use the same initial formula with a like motif for the word *Dómino* in each version, followed in 2 by a long melodic development for the surplus textual phrases. At *in aetérnum* the latter Tract agrees with *glorióse enim* of 1, in its much earlier appearance. The continuation at *adjútor* in 1, repetition of the theme at *honorificátus est*, proceeds in like manner at *qui habitat* in 2, with eliminated notes because of its shorter phrase text. A symbolic broken seventh moves upward on the word *móntes* in 2, and continues with a developed melisma to the tonal cadence, while in 1 different melodic material is used for the section starting with *Hic Déus*. This is followed by repetition of previous formulae, during which both chants meet again at *Déus pátris* in 1 and *circúitu* in 2. Following this formula there are different applications of repeated material in both versions, but they come together again, with

---

[1] W. APEL, *op. cit.*, pp. 316, 362.

slight variants, at *Dóminus nómen* of 1 and *et usque* of 2, followed by the same melismatic cadence at the close of each song.

The Requiem Mass Tract, 2) *Absólve* (1809) follows the 1) *Cantémus Dómino* version even more closely, except for the *Hic Déus* formula in 1 and its repeat at *Dóminus cónterens*. They meet again, at *Dóminus nómen* of 1 on the tonic accent of the word *beatitúdine* of 2 and except for a closing *punctum* in the latter, and a double *punctum* in 1, continue in identical settings to the end, except for a double *punctum* in 2 for two more syllables.

Similarity among the Tracts is so conspicuous that any one of them can be used as an example of comparison with a second Tract of like Mode and melodic formulae.

Melodic Procedures for Expressive and Symbolic Elements

The occasions for expressive and symbolic elements in conformity with a particular text are not as prevalent in this song as that which obtains in general in antiphonal and responsorial chant, because of the application of fixed formulae to the Tract text. However, examples of expressive and symbolic elements do exist in certain Tracts as well. In this regard, Vincent d'Indy, in his *Cours de composition musicale* (Bk. 1), describes special features in the Tract *Te Déum Pátrem* (1273). D'Indy points out the word *sólus* in this song as the key to the dogma. Accordingly, it is around this word that the most extended melisma in the entire melody is fashioned, as melodic center and support of the whole piece. Note that the first four notes of this Tract are the same as the first four notes of the Hymn *Te Déum* (1832), but in a different Mode.

Again, d'Indy offers an interesting analysis in this vein for the Tract *Ad te levávi* (554). The formula of the intonation acts as an exposition which leads up symbolically on *levávi* into the motif on *óculus* in an elevated range, as the psalmist *raises* his *eyes* to the heavens, upon the Lord. Likewise the developed melisma on the tonic accent of the word *caélis* rises symbolically to the highest point in the melody. Note the insistant modal dominant *c* at strong rhythmic points in this vocalization.

But when the eyes of the servants are on the hands of their masters and the eyes of the maid are on the hands of her mistress, the psalmist's gaze turns *downward* to earth. Accordingly, here the motif on *óculi* and its repeat descends. Then when the psalmist turns his eyes once more toward the Lord God, the original elevated motif of *óculus*, with its sequence through the cadence of *méos*, returns for *óculi nóstri* — melodic procedures with complete dramatic and symbolic effects.

Further instances of this symbolic and dramatic play may be studied in the following Tracts: *Effundérunt* (429), where the key-words *sánguinem sanctórum* rise dramatically on two soaring melismata of strong rhythm, after a calm intonation on the initial word of the song. In the Tract *Tu es vas* (1346) a remarkable melodic procedure occurs on the tonic accent of the word *intercéde*. Six consecutive times the modal dominant note *a* cries out insistently, twice as *pressus*, twice at the head of a repeated *climacus*, twice as first note of a repeated *clivis*, a constant repetition carrying with it an urgency that bodes no refusal on the part of God's chosen vessel that he *intercede* for those who implore his help.

Conclusion

If it would not seem too irrelevant that I add a word of recognition for what it appears to me is one of the most important aspects of the composition of Gregorian Chant, I would suggest that this lies in manifestation of the deep understanding the artisans of this work possessed of the religious drama of Holy Scripture, be it in the Old or New Testament. In the same manner that composers of other epochs study the librettos of the operas they are to compose, living and reliving each character until the whole has become so much a part of their very being that it in turn inspires the creative work which follows, so must our ancient authors of the Church song have meditated long and profoundly on the texts of the tremendous dramas contained in the sacred literature known as the Liturgy of the Church.

These men were not only expert musicians for their time, but they were at the same time biblical scholars and liturgists. They too knew their characters and all that bears on them and their situations. Nor was theirs an intellectual concept alone, but rather a deep spiritual insight, living and experimental, that gives their labor meaning. Everything is known exactly to the extent that this knowledge is in act. Hence, one believes that these men *lived* in some manner the various experiences and situations which they too immortalized, as well as the authors of Holy Scripture, our chant composers through the medium of song. Thus it is that the inspired product which they brought forth bears the stamp of enduring life, a fruit that has remained and that shall remain for all time.

It is, in a sense, in a like approach that we may arrive at the heart of their interpretations, so often perceived through melodic, dramatic, and symbolic elements, a fact made doubly evident through study of the most perfect union of word and melody, Gregorian Chant, the official Song of the Church.

TE DEUM LAUDAMUS

INDEX

135

Printed in Belgium by Desclée & Cie, Éditeurs, S.A., Tournai — 10.678